A Praying People

A Praying People

Essays Inspired by Dwight L. Moody

Edited by

James Spencer

and

Ashish Varma

WIPF & STOCK · Eugene, Oregon

A PRAYING PEOPLE
Essays Inspired by Dwight L. Moody

Wipf & Stock
An Imprint of Wipf and Stock Publishers
199 W. 8th Ave., Suite 3
Eugene, OR 97401

www.wipfandstock.com

PAPERBACK ISBN: 978-1-6667-6569-4
HARDCOVER ISBN: 978-1-6667-6570-0
EBOOK ISBN: 978-1-6667-6571-7

06/08/23

Contents

Introduction

By JAMES SPENCER, PHD
   and ASHISH VARMA, PHD

THE WORLD TELLS THEOLOGICAL stories of its own. If we resign ourselves to employing the logics of the world, we will surely miss opportunities to tell the world about God. In the world's theological tales, God is distorted. He is marginalized if not denied altogether. As such, the accounts the world offers are incapable of escaping the vicious loop that seeks to mitigate or follow humanity's misdirected desires through human effort. Because the people of the world do not operate in light of the truth revealed by God in Christ and through the Scriptures, they have lost sight of theological practices (such as prayer) and are left to depend on limited human wit and wisdom as they confront the complexities of human existence.

On episode 5 of Bret Weinstein's *Dark Horse* podcast, Douglas Murray, author of *The Madness of Crowds*, points toward the futility embedded within conservative and progressive movements, thereby illustrating the limits of human wisdom:

> When is it a good time to fundamentally alter an institution and when is staying with what you have a better choice? Or when can a very soft form of that change occur. . . . I don't believe in progress as a teleological force or anything like that, but obviously it's demonstrable that things get better for certain groups at certain times, certain people at certain times. But, of course, the corollary of that is that they also can get worse, which is the bit I think in the progressive vision which is always missing is that the assumption is that if you get through certain barriers it is inevitably going to get better. Whereas many things that I think progressives and

others see as forces that are holding people back are doing that and doing it for a good reason.[1]

Murray acknowledges our inability to predict the future with full certainty. Often, even our best ideas have ripple effects that create new problems. Human beings, regardless of political persuasion, gender, cultural background, or religious affiliation, are incapable of resolving the problems of the world because, apart from Christ, we have no solution to the problem of sin. While our God-given capacities and God's ongoing work among us create some sense of security, the world will not be in perfect harmony again until God creates the new heavens and new earth. Politics may well provide some stability, but the broken world needs more than the restraint of evil and the maintenance of order.

So, if conservatives are really just fighting the next battle that they are going to lose and progressives are pressing for agendas and changes that will never fix all that is wrong with the world, Christians cannot elevate anything or anyone one to the level of messiah other than Christ. How is it that the body of Christ might avoid "accepting the current state of things as 'natural' and adopting the logic of the age as our own"?[2] When both ends of the spectrum (and every position in between) are hamstrung by the crippling effects of our sinful state and incomplete understanding of the world around us, Christians must resist the urge to claim that restricted perspectives of the world are more complete than they actually are. We must fight to maintain a posture of true humility which rightly acknowledges our God-given gifts and talents *and* our deep need for the wisdom to exercise them in ways that point to God.

Israel's Journey and Our Own

When God delivered Israel from Egypt, he gave the would-be nation a legal code that would allow Israel to be a light to the nations. The law reflected God's nature. Israel was to serve the Lord alone and to reflect the Lord in their personal and national conduct (Exod 20:1–3; Deut 5:6–7). They needed no idols because the Israelite people would reflect God's glory and represent him to the world (Exod 20:4–6; Deut 5:8–10). Israel

1. Weinstein, "Douglas Murray," 13:10.
2. Spencer, *Thinking Christian*, 93.

was to represent God faithfully rather than using God to achieve their own ends (Exod 20:7; Deut 5:11).

Unlike Pharaoh, who depended on unceasing labor and military might to secure Egypt, the Lord empowers Israel to rest, to care for sojourners, and to remember that God brought them out of Egypt in more ways than one (Exod 20:8–11; Deut 5:12–15). Israel's deliverance was not only physical. It was a deliverance to a new way of life. Israel was not to become the new Egypt but to be "a kingdom of priests and a holy nation" (Exod 19:6). Yet, even over forty years in the wilderness designed to teach Israel that "man does not live on bread alone, but man lives by every word that comes from the mouth of the Lord" (Deut 8:3), Israel continued to revert back to the world's wisdom.

In the commandments, God gave Israel a set of theologically empowered instructions that underscore his sovereignty, benevolence, and wisdom. Following these statutes would not only bring life (Deut 30:15–20) but would allow Israel to worship God by obeying him and living in accordance with his law. Each commandment is rooted in the character and sovereign position of God so that:

- Honoring one's father and mother recognized God's oversight of even the basic family structure. To deny or disrespect one's parents was to suggest that God's order was somehow flawed.

- Committing murder represents the removal of a human obstacle. Whether one created in God's image is to live or die is not left to the judgement of another individual operating outside of God's established governmental structures. The life of another made in God's image is never to be sacrificed on the altar of our own selfish pursuits.

- Engaging in adultery was a denial of agreed-upon relations within society as established before God. God is not fickle, nor are covenants to be viewed as insignificant or ceremonial acts.

- Stealing suggests God could not be trusted to provide or that what God had already given was simply not enough. Taking from others diminishes God and demonstrates a lack of trust in his provision.

- Bearing false witness suggests that God's kingdom cannot execute justice when all truth is brought to life or that sustaining God's just order is less important than one's own individual desires, needs, or concerns.

- Coveting what God has given to another expresses a dissatisfaction with the manner in which God has distributed gifts amongst his people.

Even within their rich covenant relationship with the Lord, Israel was always in danger of forgetting God and adopting the practices of the nations around them. Rather than committing to obedience and trusting the Lord to care for them, the people of Israel often embraced the logics and solutions of the world to their detriment.

Faced with life in a state of sin, it can be tempting for us to dismiss God's wisdom and to chart our own course. We can become too committed to some human vision of reality that leads us to choose to do what is expedient rather than what is theological because we have fooled ourselves into thinking that the alternatives the world offers are the only alternatives available to us. *In short, it is easy for us to be shaped (individually and collectively) into the image of something other than God.* We depend upon ourselves by leaning too heavily on our own understandings and forgetting that we do not glorify God solely through the faithful use of our God-given capacities, but in our willingness to allow God's strength to be revealed through our weakness. In other words, "As we come to a fuller understanding of the kingdom by submitting all we are and have to the rule of God, the stark contrast between a life lived with God and a life lived without Him will only become more and more clear."[3]

Reorienting through Prayer

Barring an extended sojourn in the desert, how is the body of Christ to learn that "man does not live by bread alone, but man lives by every word that comes from the mouth of the Lord" (Deut 8:3)? While there are many practices in which the church might engage, prayer is surely crucial to reorienting ourselves within the world, to recognizing the possibilities that God brings, and to developing and sustaining the courage to follow God even when we don't fully understand where he is taking us. In prayer, we admit our need for guidance and support. We express our gratitude and awe for all that God has given us. We seek God for solutions we cannot see, bring about, or anticipate. We come with the recognition that the "normal" ways of being in the world may not faithfully reflect the God we serve.

3. Spencer, *Thinking Christian*, 147.

However crucial prayer may be, it isn't always apparent just how prayer functions to orient us toward the world and our activities in it. In my experience, prayer is often what I do before I do what I had already determined to do before engaging in prayer. It is not so much that I view prayer as an empty ritual, but that I am not always clear about how God might direct me through prayer. That lack of clarity is even more pronounced when the tasks that present themselves as immediate necessities squeeze out the time needed for deep, prayerful, spiritual discernment. Prayer becomes an activity I perform in the margins of my day. I give prayer the spaces that are not usefully filled with anything else when I should give it a space sufficient to express my "deep conviction that discerning the Spirit is crucial to offering faithful testimony."[4]

Rather than relegate prayer to the margins, we would be wise to immerse our days in prayer and to punctuate our days with concentrated moments of petition, adoration, gratitude, and inquiry. The reorienting power of prayer does not exist outside of the seasons and settings of life. It is one means by which we prepare ourselves for whatever seasons and settings may come. Prayer not only arises in response to the situations in which we find ourselves but is part of what allows us to understand the world in theological perspective. It is an activity that, when done in the right spirit with the right heart, can cultivate within us a faithful posture before God.

That we engage in prayer, however, is not a sure sign that we have become the sort of community capable of witnessing to God faithfully. Prayer, like other Christian disciplines, is susceptible to corruption. It is possible to pray "like the hypocrites" (Matt 6:5) or to otherwise pervert our prayers (Matt 21:13; Mark 11:17; Luke 18:10–14). Lauren Winner demonstrates some of the dangers of Christian practices by describing the practice of "family worship" in the nineteenth century. As masters or mistresses led slaves in worship, the primary aim was not worship of God but "to teach those praying about their lot in life."[5]

While prayer, like the Psalms, can often have the dual function of speaking with God and speaking to others, the challenge Winner highlights with regard to "corporate 'family' prayer (that is, prayer in which master or mistress led bondsmen and bondswomen to pray)" is that it "became principally a means of communicating something from one group of people to another, and (specifically) of reminding the subordinate

---

4. Spencer, *Thinking Christian*, chap. 11.

5. Winner, *Dangers of Christian Practice*, 67.

group of their status."[6] Prayer can communicate. It can even instruct. It should not manipulate. It is not a tool for us to sustain our preferred status quo, but a moment in which we converse with God in a way that leaves us open to transformation.

To pray well is to pray as Christ did in the garden of Gethsemane. As his suffering and death drew closer, Christ called on the Father for strength and entrusted himself to God's will. Jesus did not long to suffer. It would seem that he would have preferred that the way of "this cup" was not inevitable. Yet, Jesus surrenders to the Father's will: "My Father, if it is not possible for this cup to be taken away unless I drink it, may your will be done" (Matt 26:42).

Prayer can involve questioning, anger, frustration, confusion, lament, and a full range of other emotions. God does not desire that we hide ourselves in prayer. Based on the prayers we see in Scripture, being bold and open about what we are thinking and how we are feeling is an appropriate part of being prayerful. Whatever else is allowable in prayer, however, we do not dictate to God or others how the world should work. We are always in a posture to surrender to his will, to follow his instruction, and to allow him to work through us rather than attempting to make him work for us.

Prayer and Theology as Formative Practice

Prayer as a practice is formative, yet to be formative in the right ways, prayer must emerge from our belief that God's ways are higher than our ways (Isa 55:8-9). Prayer is a practical recognition of our own dependence on the Lord. It expresses our conviction that drawing near to God for wisdom, insight, and help is a Christian task that is as urgent as it is important. As we pray together, we acknowledge that the body of Christ is made up of incomplete people whose combined prayers inform and reinforce one another as we groan together with the "whole creation" for God's coming redemption (Rom 8:18–30).

Willie Jennings has recently advanced a similar perspective on the way God's people interact with regard to theology and theological education. Utilizing the language of "fragments," Jennings argues that theological educators need to recognize the "profound intellectual work at the heart of theological formation, that of working together in the fragments."[7] He goes

6. Winner, *Dangers*, 69.

7. Jennings, *After Whiteness*, 33.

on to suggest, "The fragment work is a deeply Christian calling, born of the tragic history of Christians who came not to learn anything from indigenous peoples but only to instruct them, and to exorcise and eradicate anything and everything that seemed strange and therefore anti-Christian."[8] Arguing that Christian work needs to account for our own incompleteness or "fragments" does not mean that theological work must accept anything and everything that people bring with them. Rather, it means that the process of coming to right theological understanding and formation is not a negligible aspect of the Christian life. Having revelation of God's great acts and direct access to the same Creator God does not mean that our thought processes, perspectives, and actions are pure and holy. Additionally, we exist and act in and from fallen places, often bearing subconscious, and fallen assumptions of normalcy. The lesson: we remain fragmented creatures who must live and can only thrive by first humbly receiving. And just as with prayer, one act of receiving is not enough. We continue humbly to receive from the source of life that is outside of ourselves.

As a practice engaged in by incomplete people, prayer is a powerful means of opening ourselves up to God's rule. As women and men with God-given talents and abilities come together, we have opportunities to utilize those gifts. Prayer does not excuse us from acting in other ways. Instead, in prayer we seek God's direction. We request that God shape our individual and collective lives by giving us the insight necessary to discern when to use our gifts and when to exercise restraint. In prayer we demonstrate our need for God's direction and our willingness to submit to his leading. We express our trust in God to act as a wise and benevolent Sovereign even when we don't fully comprehend what God is doing. As such, we may view prayer as a "human readiness to hear, to follow, to comply so that the utterly basic relationship with God can be more fully realized."[9]

Both prayer and theology are formative practices. While we often view prayer and theology as separate activities, prayer requires some level of theological understanding and doing theology requires a vibrant life of prayer. As Hauerwas notes,

> the Christian East's understanding of the theologian as a person
> of prayer continues to be a challenge to the dominant forms of
> theology developed since the Reformation. Of course, theologians
> in the West may pray, but they do not necessarily do theology as

8. Jennings, *After Whiteness*, 37.

9. Chan, *Spiritual Theology*, 129.

a form of prayer. I think we quite literally do not know how that is to be done.[10]

Though Hauerwas is primarily concerned with the work of academic theologians, the body of Christ is a theological community doing the sort of theology that may be described as "faith seeking understanding of everyday life."[11] As such, all of us would do well to wrestle with what it might mean to "do theology as a form of prayer."

Doing theology as a form of prayer suggests that "faith seeking understanding of everyday life" is an activity done in community with God and others. Karl Barth notes, "It is a great thing to preach, to believe, and to fulfill our small obedience to God's commandments. But in all these forms of obedience and faith it is prayer that puts us in rapport with God and permits us to collaborate with him."[12] Perhaps one of the challenges we have in understanding theology as a form of prayer is that we think of theology as a product as opposed to an ongoing process.

Surely, we have doctrinal anchors to which we tether ourselves so as not to drift off into heresy. Acknowledging that theology is a process does not deny the surety of doctrine. It is not a move toward relative truth. Instead, it recognizes there is always more of God to discover as we plumb the depths of his word and walk with him in the concrete experiences of our lives. As we engage in the theological process by which we "seek, speak, and show understanding of what God was doing in Christ for the sake of the world," we also allow our understandings of God to be subject to ongoing analysis and scrutiny knowing that the task of theology involves reform.[13]

The unending task of theology contributes to what it might mean for theology to be done as a form of prayer in so much as theology so understood is incomplete. Theology is a series of moments in which we submit our understandings to God with the implicit request that he give depth and nuance to even our most faithful interpretations of the biblical text. In doing theology, we make assertions, but our assertions should always be accompanied by the hope that our fellows within the body of Christ will contribute their own understandings of God so that we can speak more faithfully about God together. Beyond making assertions, theology's unfinished-ness makes the theological task a form of prayer at least to the extent

10. Hauerwas, *Work of Theology*, 110.

11. Vanhoozer, *Everyday Theology*, 17.

12. Barth, *Prayer*, 20.

13. Vanhoozer and Strachan, *Pastor as Public Theologian*, 17.

that our assertions, however true, are not complete. Theology is, after all, an activity which requires that we "take God himself seriously in the study by making our study an encounter with him."[14]

In some sense, then, the lines between theology and prayer are blurred because, as we do theology, we are encountering God, and as we pray, we converse with God to develop eyes that see more clearly and ears that hear more keenly just what God is doing in our lives and in the world. In both activities we open ourselves up to God and seek to be conformed ever more closely to the image of Christ. While prayer and theology can reinforce our understanding of the world, we do not pray *or engage in theology* without some expectation that God will transform us. As Vanhoozer notes, "Prayer, like doctrine itself, is a powerful tonic of reality, exposing our artificial psychological and social constructions to be no more than glittering images, a theater of shadows."[15] Prayer, in other words, reorients us by placing us in a position to see the world from new angles.

Organization of this Book

Written as a festschrift of sorts to the nineteenth-century evangelist D. L. Moody, this collection of essays explores a topic that was crucial to Dwight Moody's life and ministry. As Moody notes, "God's best gifts, like valuable jewels, are kept under lock and key, and those who want them must, with fervent faith, importunately ask for them; for God is the rewarder of them that diligently seek Him." It is in that spirit that these essays are offered to God's people as a humble attempt to contribute to our collective understanding of prayer. More than that, they are offered in the hope that God's people will learn to pray together in ways that shape us into women and men capable of reflecting God's glory in a dark world.

The first two essays in this book interact with Mr. Moody's understanding of prayer. Gregg Quiggle's essay offers an overview of D. L. Moody and prayer while James Spencer considers Moody's understanding of prayer as a perilous activity in which we surrender ourselves to God's will. The rest of the included essays offer unique biblical and theological insights into prayer through the analysis of key historical figures and biblical and theological themes. Lindsey Hankins provides a sweeping account of prayer offering personal insights alongside those made by the likes of

14. Averbeck, "God, People, and the Bible," 155.

15. Vanhoozer, *Drama of Doctrine*, 394.

Origen, Augustine, and Gregory of Nyssa. The essays of May Young and Bryan Babcock offer analyses of lament as a crucial form of prayer. Grace Hamman recovers for us the significant Medieval voice of Julian of Norwich, demonstrating the way that our prayer flows from grasping God's prior and greatest prayer in the giving of Jesus Christ. Ashish Varma then delves into the deep connections between prayer and the material world, working with biblical themes and the work of Tolkien. Drawing on her own Kenyan background and biblical and theological acumen, Stephanie Lowery argues that prayer is both communion and communication, highlighting the intimacy involved as we engage in prayer.

These essays do not exhaust all that might be said about prayer. We are not attempting to close the book on this important topic. Rather, we seek to offer encouragement to a church that is to be a people of prayer. We pray that as you engage with the essays in this book you will be inspired to consider your own prayer life and to challenge your sisters and brothers in Christ to become a praying people.

Bibliography

Averbeck, Richard. "God, People, and the Bible: The Relationship between Illumination and Biblical Scholarship." In *Who's Afraid of the Holy Spirit? An Investigation into the Ministry of the Spirit of God Today*, edited by Daniel B. Wallace and M. James Sawyer, 137–66. Dallas: Biblical Studies, 2005.

Barth, Karl. *Prayer.* Louisville: Westminster John Knox, 2002.

Chan, Simon. *Spiritual Theology: A Systematic Study of the Christian Life.* Downers Grove: InterVarsity, 1998.

Hauerwas, Stanley. *The Work of Theology.* Grand Rapids: Eerdmans, 2015.

Jennings, Willie James. *After Whiteness: An Education in Belonging.* Grand Rapids: Eerdmans, 2020.

Spencer, James. *Thinking Christian: Essays on Testimony, Accountability, and the Christian Mind.* N.p.: Self-published, 2020.

Vanhoozer, Kevin J. *The Drama of Doctrine: A Canonical-Linguistic Approach to Christian Theology.* Louisville: Westminster John Knox, 2005.

———. *Everyday Theology: How to Read Cultural Texts and Interpret Trends.* Grand Rapids: Baker, 2007.

Vanhoozer, Kevin J., and Owen Strachan. *The Pastor as Public Theologian: Reclaiming a Lost Vision.* Grand Rapids: Baker, 2015.

Weinstein, Bret. "Douglas Murray." *Dark Horse* (podcast), October 16, 2019. https://podcasts.apple.com/us/podcast/bret-weinstein-darkhorse-podcast/id1471581521?i=1000459815269.

Winner, Lauren F. *The Dangers of Christian Practice: On Wayward Gifts, Characteristic Damage, and Sin.* New Haven: Yale University Press, 2018.

Moody and Prayer

By GREGG QUIGGLE, PhD

He who kneels the most, stands the best.

—DWIGHT MOODY

ALONG WITH HIS FRIEND Charles Spurgeon, Dwight Moody would dominate the English-speaking evangelical world throughout the mid and late nineteenth century. A truly transatlantic figure, Moody was arguably as influential in the United Kingdom as his native United States. His life and work would be front-page news until his death in 1899. Although remembered primarily as an evangelist, Moody was an educator, a leader in forming Christian publishing, and active in building movements to address the urban social ills of his day. His life would span the American Civil War and the so-called Gilded Age. This was a period marked by massive immigration, industrialization, and urbanization. It was an age of sharp contrasts featuring the great industrialists like Carnegie, Vanderbilt, and Rockefeller and enormous slums in burgeoning urban centers. It was an age that was marked by considerable increases in technology and mechanization.

Moody would cast a long shadow after his death. It is hardly an overstatement to claim he was the founder of modern evangelicalism. Perhaps these two observations capture his legacy best. The historian Martin Marty stated Dwight Moody could simply have been called "Mr. Revivalist and perhaps even Mr. Protestant."[1] And the great evangelist of our previous generation Billy Graham consciously patterned his ministry after Mr. Moody. In discussing Moody's legacy, Graham once wrote to Dwight Moody's daughter, "I am wondering if you all are really aware of

1. Marty, "Foreword," 1.

the many movements that now exist throughout the world that flowed from the ministry of Dwight Moody."[2]

Prayer was one of the central features of Moody's life and ministry.[3] In 1923, one of Dwight Lyman Moody's closest associates, R. A. Torrey, preached a sermon titled, "Why God Used D. L. Moody." In the sermon, Torrey gave seven reasons why God used Mr. Moody. One of the seven Torrey identified was that "Mr. Moody was in the deepest and most meaningful sense a man of prayer." Torrey went on to say, "Yes, D. L. Moody certainly was a wonderful preacher; taking it all in all, the most wonderful preacher I have ever heard, and it was a great privilege to hear him preach as he alone could preach; but out of a very intimate acquaintance with him I wish to testify that he was a far greater prayer than he was a preacher."[4]

After Moody's death, there was a time for personal testimony on the campus. One student, who worked with Moody, rose and gave the following testimony, confirming Torrey's assertion:

> I should like to speak especially of the place that prayer had in his life. I have been looking through some of his letters lately, letters which I received from him during these years that I have been at Northfield, and there is scarcely one of them in which there is not some mention of prayer. Sometimes he wrote asking me to pray for the work in a certain city, that the ground might be ready for the seed; again, he would write that he was to speak upon the Atonement or upon the Holy Spirit, and would ask me to pray that God would make it real to the people; then there would come letters saying that the work was deepening, that he believed it was in answer to prayer.[5]

Moody always demanded intensely focused prayer in preparation for his revival campaigns.

When he began new projects, he often called on the students and faculty of his schools to devote themselves to fasting and prayer. Emphasizing the importance and power of prayer was so crucial to Moody it was one of the predominant characteristics of his schools in both Northfield and Chicago.

2. Powell Family Collection, Moody Center Archives, Northfield, MA.

3. I am particularly indebted to Rodney Baker's study on the impact on prayer on Mr. Moody's life and ministry. This work provided unique insights and helpful resources that helped shape my understanding. Baker, "Impact of Prayer."

4. Torrey, *Why God Used D. L. Moody.*

5. Moody, *Life of Dwight L. Moody,* 582.

D. L. Moody not only worked hard for the Lord, but he also prayed hard as he worked. His student conferences in Northfield featured 6:00 a.m. prayer meetings, and he organized prayer meetings for children. Later, he would say that "Some of the happiest nights I ever had were in these children's prayer meetings."[6] His life and enduring work stand as an eloquent testimony to the fruits of fervent prayer.

Moody practiced what he preached when home. He rose before the family to pray and study the Bible.[7] But Moody's home prayer life was not just personal. After the family breakfasted, Moody would bring them all together for a period of Bible reading and prayer.[8] By some accounts, throughout the day, he would interrupt playtime with his children and call them to get on their knees to pray.[9] Moody seamlessly wove prayer into the daily family activities.

His approach to prayer is best captured by his 1884 book *Prevailing Prayer: What Hinders It?* The book is typical Moody. It combines Bible teaching, practical instruction with numerous antidotes and sentimental stories. For a complete picture of Moody's approach to prayer, I highly recommend it. This essay will try to present an overview of Moody's understanding of and commitment to prayer. Specifically, I will examine the impact of prayer on Moody's life and ministry, the factors that shaped his understanding of prayer, and his practice of and advice about prayer.

The Formation of a Man of Prayer

Moody was born in February of 1837 to Edwin and Betsy Moody in the small town of Northfield, Massachusetts. Northfield is nestled on the east side of the Connecticut River in the rolling rural hills of Western Massachusetts, only a few miles south of the Vermont and New Hampshire borders. The house of Moody's youth is a simple two-story white clapboard structure sitting on one of the ridges on the north side of the town.

The Moody family was large and financially vulnerable. The Father, Edwin, was a stonemason and, by some accounts, a drinker. The family was in debt, the extent of which became evident as with Edwin's unexpected death in 1841. Edwin returned early from work complaining of abdominal pain.

6. Moody, *Life of Dwight L. Moody*, 108.

7. Moody, *My Father*, 50.

8. Moody and Fitt, *Shorter Life of D. L. Moody*, 91.

9. Nason, *Lives of the Eminent American Evangelists*, 86.

The pain increased quickly, and he died later in the day. The family debt load was severe enough that by the end of the day that Edwin died, debt collectors had already removed many of the goods from their home. At Edwin's death, Dwight was only four years old and one of seven. This was compounded by his mother being eight months pregnant with twins.

Before the tragedy, there is little evidence of the family's involvement in any local churches. Edwin's death would be the catalyst for change. Shortly after Edwin's death, the family's plight became known to the Reverend Oliver Everett, pastor of the town's Unitarian church. Everett cared for the family and became a father figure to Dwight. Everett impacted the family such that they became regular church attenders, and the children were enrolled in Sunday School. In addition to being Moody's introduction to the church, the tragedy would also prove to be Dwight's first lesson in prayer. Dwight Moody's initial instruction in prayer came from watching his mother.

In these early years, we know little about Betsy's religious conviction. But we know she prayed and prayed in a manner that marked her children. For Dwight, his mother seems to be his first exposure to consistent prayer. It is clear her practice impressed him. Before his death, Edwin had given a Bible to Betsy. One of Dwight's siblings described how this Bible and prayer came to play a role in her life. She describes hearing Betsy weeping and praying over the Bible. Later the child would look at the Bible and found her mother had marked Jer 49:1, "Leave thy fatherless children, I will preserve them alive, and let thy widows trust in me." Betsy anchored her soul on this text and taught her children to pray to God, believing he would care for the orphan and widow. Dwight recalled moments when Betsy became overwhelmed with managing the children. He said she would head off to her room to pray for wisdom and patience, pleading with God to help her keep order in the family. Speaking at her funeral, Moody also often recalled awakening and hearing his mother pouring out her burdens to God in prayer.

Betsy's example during his childhood stayed with Moody throughout his life. Moody learned to turn to the Lord in prayer. He saw how prayer sustained his mother and brought her and the family through incredibly daunting events. He saw the peace prayer brought to her soul. Moody took these lessons to heart, becoming etched into his soul.

The second crucial event came after he moved to Chicago. As a teenager, he tired of life in Northfield and headed to Boston to seek his fortune.

In Boston, Moody was first confronted with the claims of the gospel through his kindly Sunday School teacher, Edward Kimball. While Boston was the context for Moody's conversion, it is in Chicago that his faith took root. Chicago would also be the context of his second lesson on prayer.

While in Chicago, Moody became involved in what has become known as the "Businessman's Revival" or the "Prayer Meeting Revival." The revival began with a series of prayer meetings directed toward business people in New York City. It would sweep across the business communities in major cities running from 1857 to 1860. When the meeting arrived in Chicago, Moody immediately became involved. He penned the following note to his mother. "There is a great revival of religion in this city. I go to meeting every night. Oh, how I do enjoy it! It seems as if God were here Himself. Oh, Mother, pray for us. Pray that this work may go on until every knee is bowed. I wish there could be a revival in Northfield."[10] The Chicago revival led to the development of a regular noon prayer meeting. Moody was critical in its formation and would eventually be appointed its leader.[11] James Edwin Orr, a distinguished researcher of revivals, describes a conversation he had with another historian. The other scholar asked if Moody started the revival; Orr replied, "[N]o, Moody did not start the '58 Revival. The '58 Revival started Moody."[12] At least, as far as his prayer life goes, that statement is accurate. Orr even further states, "Moody was without question the greatest single product of the Revival."[13] Commenting on the effect of these meetings just before his death, Moody remarked, "I would like before I go hence to see the whole church of God quickened as it was in '57."[14]

What is significant is how this revival began and spread. Prayer meetings led by laypeople drove it. As we have seen, Moody admired this movement. Through the revival, Moody saw the entire nation affected. While his mother's example demonstrated the impact of prayer personally, this revival showed how prayer could impact a whole society. Given Moody's comments during the revival and his nostalgic reflections about the revival towards the end of his life, it is apparent he looked to it as a model for his ministry.

---

10. Findlay, *American Evangelist*, 63; Moody, *Life of Dwight L. Moody*, 48.

11. Moody, *Life of Dwight L. Moody*, 115.

12. Orr, "Revival and Evangelism," 6. See also McDow and Reid, *Firefall*, 265–67.

13. Orr, *Fervent Prayer*, 200.

14. D. L. Moody, quoted in Orr, *Fervent Prayer*, 198.

A third experience also happens in Chicago. Living in a boarding house, Moody befriended the godly owner Mrs. H. Phillips, or "Mother" Phillips as she was commonly known. Phillips was a stalwart at the First Baptist Church and a woman of prayer. During Moody's time with her, she schooled Moody on the necessity of faithful prayer. Cumulatively, these three experiences shaped Moody. Moody took those lessons to heart and developed a consistent prayer life.

There is significant evidence of Moody's deepening understanding of the importance of prayer. A letter to his mother in 1858 reveals his burden for prayer. Moody pleads for prayer on his behalf, for the lost young men of the city, and for the ability to witness to those young men around him.[15] As his life continued, Moody repeatedly talked about the importance of prayer. He wrote, "[N]othing is more pleasing to our Father in heaven than direct, importunate, and persevering prayer."[16]

In his book *Prevailing Prayer*, Moody begins his first chapter with the following sentence: "Those who have left the deepest impression on this sin-cursed earth have been men and women of prayer."[17] With this statement, Moody explained his ministry. It is no accident that those around him noted the connection between Moody's prayer and his Christian service. Moody's eloquence or education cannot explain his success. Moody's education was limited; he received about five years of formal education. His grammar was atrocious. While speaking to the students at Cambridge University, he began, "Young gentlemen, don't ever think God don't love you, for he do!" His preaching was equally unpolished. One described his sermons as, "[there is a] scuffle among the words for suitable places in his hasty sentences; they become chipped and mutilated. Final letters disappear, middle syllables are elided, and the outer ones run together.[18] Another, "His gestures, like his rate of utterance, were subdued at first, but by the time he had warmed to his subject—and in never more than five minutes—he was vigorous, sometimes violent, speaking at an occasional clip of 230 words a minute . . . to the despair of stenographic reporters.[19] C. H. Spurgeon once remarked that Moody was "the only man who could say

---

15. Moody, *Life of Dwight L. Moody,* 53.

16. Moody, *Prevailing Prayer,* 99.

17. Moody, *Prevailing Prayer,* 7.

18. Findlay, *American Evangelist,* 223.

19. Curtis, *They Called Him Mister Moody,* 192.

'Mesopotamia' in two syllables.[20] In commenting on the impact of Moody's preaching, one of Moody's companions, R. A. Torrey, often said, "Moody is a far greater prayer than a preacher."[21] Moody confirmed this description, he put it this way: "There must be more prayer, more heart-searching, more going into the closet and closing the door, there meeting God face to face, to obtain power to present the love of God in a fitting manner to the multitudes."[22] Over and over again, Moody spoke of the fact that the power for Christian service could only come through prayer. It was only here the effects of the work could be secured. The secret, as Moody put it, was "the Spirit of the living God, co-operating specially with the spirit of the speaker, and preparing the minds of those that hear for the reception of the truth." As he put it, "The Holy Ghost is here in power. . . . God is with me: this is all the strength I have."[23] As one commentator summarized it best, "Prayer was the real working power of Moody's life."[24]

The Content of Moody's Prayers

Indeed, Moody prays for the kinds of things we all pray about: sickness, grief, work, protection, lost friends and relatives, etc. However, one of the unique themes of Moody's prayers was to be empowered by the Holy Spirit. He expressed this clearly in one of his published sermons. "Let us pray that God will fill us with the Holy Ghost. Let us pray that He will send the Spirit into our cold churches and Sabbath-schools, that are now so stiff and formal. . . . Let us pray to the God of Elijah and let us pray that the fire may come down and bum up all the dross in our hearts—all that is not pleasing in the sight of God—and that we may be filled with the Holy Spirit."[25]

Moody had seen the impact of praying for the Holy Spirit in his own life. Two women, Sarah Cooke and Mrs. W. R. Haxwurst, attended a Free

---

20. George, *Mr. Moody and the Evangelical Tradition*, 2.

21. Albus, *Treasury of Dwight L. Moody*, 38.

22. Albus, *Treasury of Dwight L. Moody*, 35.

23. Nason, *Lives of the Eminent American Evangelists*, 229–30.

24. Rowe, *D. L. Moody*, 80.

25. Moody, *Ten Days with D. L. Moody*, 141–42. Moody's conception of "baptism in the Holy Spirit" has been the source of much debate. It is well beyond the scope of this essay to address that issue. Suffice to say, after significant reading on the subject, I am convinced Moody meant being filled with the Holy Spirit, not a second work as is promoted in the Pentecostal traditions.

Methodist camp meeting during the summer of 1871. During one of the meetings, Cooke reported that "a burden came upon me for Mr. Moody, that the Lord would give him the Baptism of the Holy Ghost and of fire."[26] After listening to Moody preach for weeks, they approached him and told him, "We have been praying for you." Somewhat miffed, Moody replied, "Why don't you pray for the people?" Their response was, "Because you need the power of the Spirit." Moody recalled thinking, "I need the power! Why," said Mr. Moody, "I thought I had power. I had the largest congregations in Chicago, and there were many conversions. I was in a sense satisfied."[27]

However, the women kept up their prayer vigil and constantly urged him to seek special power from the Holy Spirit.[28] Eventually, persuaded of their sincerity, Moody agreed to sit down with the women. According to Torrey, the women introduced Moody to the concept of baptism in the Holy Spirit.[29] Because of that conversation, Moody agreed to pray with the women concerning the matter. He described the event in the following manner: "There came a great hunger into my soul. I did not know what it was. I began to cry out, as I never did before. I really felt that I did not want to live if I could not have this power for service."[30] Cooke described Moody as being in such great agony "that he rolled on the floor and in the midst of many tears and groans cried to God to be baptized with the Holy Ghost and fire."[31]

His quest finally came to a head in New York City in 1871. Here is how he described it:

> Well, one day, in the city of New York—oh what a day! I cannot describe it; I seldom refer to it; it is almost too sacred an experience to name. Paul had an experience of which he never spoke for fourteen years. I can only say that God revealed Himself to me, and I had such an experience of His love that I had to ask Him to stay His hand. I went to preaching again. The sermons were not

26. Cooke, *Wayside Sketches*, 393.

27. Moody, *Life of Dwight L. Moody*, 146. See also Torrey, *Why God Used D. L. Moody*, 45–46.

28. Cooke, *Wayside Sketches*, 393.

29. Torrey, *Why God Used D. L. Moody*, 45, 46. It should be noted that what is referred to as "baptism in the Holy Spirit" by Torrey and Moody is different than the Pentecostal conception. For Moody and Torrey, "baptism in the Holy Spirit" is a filling for power for Christian service, not the impartation of the gift of tongues.

30. Quoted in Moody, *Life of Dwight L. Moody*, 147.

31. Cooke, *Wayside Sketches*, 393.

different; I did not present any new truths, and yet hundreds were converted. I would not now be placed back where I was before that blessed experience if you should give me all the world—it would be as the small dust of the balance.[32]

Prayer for the power of the Holy Spirit became a consistent theme in his life. He once remarked, "I'd rather die than not have the power of God on my life to work for Him. I'd rather die than live for the sake of living."[33] Again and again, Moody pled with God for the Holy Spirit to work in his life and ministry.

Moody's Method of Prayer

Despite his intense emphasis on prayer, Moody never separated prayer and Bible study. He insisted they be linked. Not that they should be done together, but that one should not take the place of the other. As he put it,

> It is by the Word that the Father sanctifies us; but we are also bidden to watch and pray, lest we enter into temptation. These two means of grace must be used in their right proportion. If we read the Word and do not pray, we may become puffed up with knowledge, without the love that buildeth up. If we pray without reading the Word, we shall be ignorant of the mind and will of God, and become mystical and fanatical, and liable to be blown about by every wind of doctrine.[34]

The same directness and brevity that marked Moody's sermons were displayed in his prayer life. His son Paul noted he was often surprised by the shortness of Moody's prayers.[35] Many would be surprised to hear Moody never spent an entire night in prayer. He admitted he had tried but was unable.[36] Two events illustrate Moody's approach to prayer. One New Year's Day, Moody commenced visiting two hundred families in his congregation. One of the onlookers described his approach as follows. Bounding to the front door, Moody would greet the family with, "You know me: I am Moody; this is Deacon Thane, this is Brother Hitchcock. Are you all well? Do you all come

---

32. Moody, *Life of Dwight L. Moody*, 149. Also, Fitt, *Moody Still Lives*, 28–29; and Gericke, *Crucial Experiences*, 39–45.

33. Moody, *Secret Power*, 113.

34. Moody, *Prevailing Prayer*, 9.

35. Moody, *My Father*, 97.

36. Moody, *My Father*, 97.

to church and Sunday-School? Have you all the coal you need for the winter? Let us pray." And down we would go upon our knees, while Mr. Moody offered from fifteen to twenty words of earnest, tender, sympathetic supplication, that God would bless the man, his wife, and each one of the children. Having completed his visit, he was off to the next place. The observer noted the whole process took about a minute and a half.[37]

The second and most stunning example comes from Moody's brush with death while making an Atlantic crossing on the steamer *Spree*. The ship suffered a mechanical failure and for two days drifted, taking on water. Gripped by fear, many gathered on the deck for a night of prayer. Moody, however, remained below asleep. A rescue ship appeared about two o'clock in the morning, and Moody was awakened. Later, a passenger confronted him about not being part of the prayer meeting. Moody's reply was short and instructive. He simply stated, "I'm all prayed up."[38]

In the previously mentioned *Prevailing Prayer*, Moody noted the brevity of prayers found in the Bible. Moody concluded what mattered to God was sincerity and earnestness, not length. That does not mean Moody did not carry on a sort of informal running conversations with the Lord throughout the day. But it did mean Moody believed that when we are focused on God in prayer—in prevailing prayer—we are to be precise and clear. That is more important than length.

When instructing others on praying, Moody presents a list of nine elements that are essential to prayer. Here is how he describes them in *Prevailing Prayer*:

> The first is Adoration; we cannot meet God on a level at the start. We must approach Him as One far beyond our reach or sight. The next is Confession; sin must be put out of the way. We cannot have communion with God while there is any transgression between us. If there stands some wrong you have done a man, you cannot expect that man's favor until you go to him and confess the fault. Restitution is another; we have to make good the wrong, wherever possible. Thanksgiving is the next; we must be thankful for what God has done for us already. Then comes Forgiveness, and then Unity; and then for prayer, such as these things produce, there must be Faith. Thus influenced, we shall be ready to offer a direct Petition. We hear a good deal of praying that is just exhorting, and if you did not see the man's eyes closed,

37. Daniels, *D. L Moody and His Work*, 116.
38. Buttrick, *Prayer*, 194.

you would suppose he was preaching. Then, much that is called prayer is simply finding fault. There needs to be more petition in our prayers. After all these, there must come Submission. While praying, we must be ready to accept the will of God.[39]

Within each of these nine categories, we find unique insight from Mr. Moody. It is outside the scope of this chapter to delve into each of these categories. However, there are a few sections worth emphasizing.

Adoration is the first category. Moody begins the chapter on adoration by noting how much that we call "adoration" is self-oriented. Citing a Reverend Newman Hall, Moody points out much of our adoration is simply reciting to God all he has done for us. He concludes, "Like Jacob at Bethel, we are disposed to make the worship we render to God correlative with 'food to eat, and raiment to put on.'"[40] Moody argues adoration should be solely God-directed, centered on who he is, not what he has done for us. As if to amplify the point, Moody ends with an unattributed poem on the Trinity.[41] This caution seems particularly relevant, given the short shrift this truth about God is given in our preaching and prayers.

While discussing the category of confession, Moody begins by stating that his discussion is not focused on unbelievers but rather Christians. Connecting confession and prayer, Moody asserts, "If you go back to the Scripture records, you will find that the men who lived nearest to God, and had most power with Him, were those who confessed their sins and failures."[42] He then quickly demolishes the notion that believers have nothing to confess. Appealing to Daniel, Moody writes, "Daniel, as we have seen, confessed his sins and those of his people. Yet there is nothing recorded against Daniel. He was one of the best men then on the face of the earth yet was his confession of sin one of the deepest and most humble on record."[43]

What is impressive here is not that Moody presents new thoughts or develops new insights. Instead, Moody builds a unique argument by placing piece upon piece of Bible stories and texts to form a stack of commands and illustrations. Over and over, he shows how Christians sin and desperately need to confess daily to the Lord, and this confession must be sincere. He cites his friend Spurgeon's comments on the prayer of Pharoah,

---

39. Moody, *Prevailing Prayer*, 34, 35.

40. Moody, *Prevailing Prayer*, 40.

41. Moody, *Prevailing Prayer*, 48, 49.

42. Moody, *Prevailing Prayer*, 51.

43. Moody, *Prevailing Prayer*, 51.

"Entreat the Lord that He may take away the frogs from me." Spurgeon remarks, "A fatal flaw is manifest in that prayer. It contains no confession of sin. He says not, 'I have rebelled against the Lord; entreat that I may find forgiveness!' Nothing of the kind; he loves sin as much as ever. A prayer without penitence is a prayer without acceptance."[44]

Confession was vital because Moody was convinced sin impeded the Holy Spirit. Having seen Moody's understanding of the critical nature of the Holy Spirit's role in the believer's life, this emphasis is hardly surprising. As Moody put it, "I believe many a man is praying to God to fill him when he is full already with something else. Before we pray that God will fill us, I believe we ought to pray for Him to empty us."[45]

Moody transitions into arguably the most unique chapter in *Prevailing Prayer*: "Restitution." Moody begins by reminding the reader of the story of Zacchaeus. When Zacchaeus meets Christ, he is convicted of his sin. But he does more than confess; he pledges to give half his riches to the poor and give back to everyone he has stolen from fourfold. What Moody is pointing out is confession alone is not enough. He writes, "If I have at any time taken what does not belong to me, and am not willing to make restitution, my prayers will not go very far toward heaven. It is a singular thing, but I have never touched on this subject in my addresses without hearing of immediate results."[46] He goes even further, "If there is true repentance it will bring forth fruit. If we have done wrong to someone, we should never ask God to forgive us until we are willing to make restitution. If I have done any man a great injustice and can make it good, I need not ask God to forgive me until I am willing to do so."[47] Again, we see Moody's commitment to the Holy Spirit's critical work in the believer's life. He maintains that as we confess and open our hearts to God the Holy Spirit, God will cause us to understand we need to make things right.

While Moody believes making restitution to those, we have wronged is vital, he also believes forgiving those who have wronged us is equally vital. As he put it, "The next thing is perhaps the most difficult of all to deal with—Forgiveness. I believe this is keeping more people from having power with God than any other thing—they are not willing to cultivate the Spirit of Forgiveness. If we allow the root of bitterness to spring up in our hearts against

44. Moody, *Prevailing Prayer*, 58.

45. Moody, *Secret Power*, 32.

46. Moody, *Prevailing Prayer*, 78.

47. Moody, *Prevailing Prayer*, 76.

someone, our prayer will not be answered."[48] As Moody sees it, bitterness blocks communion with God. But he goes even further; He reminds us of the teachings of Jesus in chapter 5 of Matthew's Gospel. There Jesus says if you are making an offering to God and remember a brother or sister has something against you, go to that person and seek to be reconciled. Moody's point is that prayer is hindered when we live a life filled with conflict with others in the faith. We must go the extra mile to find peace among each other. For Moody, our vertical relationship with God through prayer is tied to our horizontal relationships with the family of faith.

Lessons from Mr. Moody

As we look at Mr. Moody, it becomes evident why he was so influential in his time. It is not his eloquence or intellect. What stands out is his honesty, earnestness, and practicality. These characteristics flow from God-given genius and prayer.

So, what does Mr. Moody teach us that we can apply to our lives today? First, some of us worry too much about the length of time we spend in prayer. Moody reminds us that focus and earnestness are more important than length. As Moody pointed out, most of the prayers we find in the Bible are short. What we call the "Lord's Prayer" is not very long.

Additionally, Moody's advice makes sense based on our experience with our fellow humans if you think about it. We would all rather have an earnest and direct conversation than a long rambling conversation where our attention is constantly wavering. The Lord certainly deserves our full attention. However, this is not to say there is anything wrong with extended periods of prayer. It is to say numerous short, focused prayers are acceptable to the Lord. It is also not to say an ongoing informal conversation with God is wrong. It is to say; there must be times of concentrated prayer.

Moody also reminds us we are Trinitarian—we confess, as the old hymn puts it, "God in three persons blessed Trinity."[49] While centering on Christ is proper, He did not act independently, and we confess belief in the Triune God. Practically, I have found it helpful to thank each member of the Trinity for their roles in my salvation. For example, thank the Father for planning for our salvation, remember Jesus did the Father's will. Thank the Son for his suffering, death, and resurrection that secured our salvation.

48. Moody, *Prevailing Prayer*, 106.
49. Heber, "Holy, Holy, Holy," 2.

Finally, thank the Spirit for testifying to the Son by forming the Bible and drawing us to the Son through his witness in the text.

Mr. Moody's emphasis on adoration is timely and practical. Rarely in human history has there been such an emphasis on the individual. Being true to yourself and seeking your way is the rallying cry of our time. We are people who tend to think it is all about me. Consequently, too often, what we call adoration is self-centered. Specifically, we confuse thankfulness with adoration. Often, we spend most of our time thanking God for what he has done for us, rather than praising him for who he is! Try praising God for his wisdom, power, and knowledge during your prayers.

Moody's linking of confession and restitution is both unique and instructive. In some ways, by linking the two, Moody gets to one of the most challenging elements of confession—sincerity. At times it is hard to read our hearts. Are we genuinely sorry or just trying to avoid punishment? Is our repentance genuine? Making restitution requires a much deeper commitment than simply saying you are sorry. The next time you pray, consider asking the Lord to guide you into identifying ways you may need to make restitution to those you have hurt or defrauded.

But perhaps the most important lesson from Mr. Moody is to remind us of the necessity of prayer. Prayer is a remarkable example of God's love and grace. Think of it: at any instant, we can talk to the Triune God, and he listens! May God grant us the grace to seek of face God regularly and earnestly in prayer.

Bibliography

Albus, Harry J. *A Treasury of Dwight L. Moody.* Grand Rapids: Eerdmans, 1949.

Baker, Rodney. "The Impact of Prayer on the Ministries of D. L. Moody, C. H. Spurgeon, and Billy Graham: A Descriptive Study." DMin diss., Liberty University, 1999.

Buttrick, George Arthur. *Prayer.* New York: Abingdon-Cokesbury, 1942.

Cooke, Sarah. *Wayside Sketches: or, The Handmaiden of the Lord.* Grand Rapids: Shaw, 1895.

Curtis, Richard K. *They Called Him Mr. Moody.* New York: Doubleday, 1962.

Daniels, W. H. *D. L. Moody and His Work.* Hartford: American, 1875.

Dorsett, Lyle. *A Passion for Souls: The Life of D. L. Moody.* Chicago: Moody, 1997.

Findlay, James. *Dwight L. Moody: American Evangelist, 1837–1899.* Chicago: University of Chicago Press, 1969.

Fitt, A. P. *Moody Still Lives: Word Pictures of D. L. Moody.* Philadelphia: Pinebrook Book Club, 1936.

———. *A Shorter Life of D. L. Moody.* Chicago: Bible Institute Colportage Association, 1900.

George, Timothy. ed. *Mr. Moody and the Evangelical Tradition.* New York: T. & T. Clark, 2004.

Gericke, Paul. *Crucial Experiences in the Life of D. L. Moody.* New Orleans: Insight, 1978.

Heber, Reginald. "Holy, Holy, Holy! Lord God Almighty." In *The Worshiping Church Hymnal,* edited by Donald P. Hustad, 2. Carol Stream, IL: Hope Publishing Company, 1990.

Marty, Martin. "Foreword." In *Dwight L. Moody: American Evangelist, 1837–1899,* 1–4. Chicago: University of Chicago Press, 1969.

McDow, Malcolm, and Alvin L. Reid. *Firefall: How God Has Shaped History Through Revivals.* Nashville: Broadman & Holman, 1997.

Moody, D. L. *Prevailing Prayer: What Hinders It?* Chicago: Revell, 1884.

———. *Secret Power: A Secret of Success in Christian Life and Work.* Chicago: Revell, 1881.

———. *Ten Days with D. L. Moody, Comprising a Collection of His Sermons.* New York: Ogilvie, 1886.

Moody, Paul D. *My Father.* Boston: Little, Brown, 1938.

Moody, Paul D., and Arthur Percy Fitt. *The Shorter Life of D. L. Moody.* Chicago: Bible Institute Colportage Association, 1900.

Moody, William. *The Life of Dwight L. Moody.* New York: Macmillan, 1930.

Nason, Elias. *The Lives of the Eminent American Evangelists, Dwight L. Moody, and Ira D. Sankey: With an Account of Their Work in England and America.* Boston: Lothrup & Russell, 1877.

Orr, James Edwin. "Revival and Evangelism." *World Evangelization Information Bulletin* 38 (1985) 6–10.

———. *The Fervent Prayer: The Worldwide Impact of the Great Awakening of 1858.* Chicago: Moody, 1974.

Rowe, A. T. *D. L. Moody: The Soul-Winner.* Anderson, IN: Gospel Trumpet, 1927.

Torrey, R. A. *Why God Used D. L. Moody.* Chicago: The Bible Institute Colportage Association, 1923.

The Perilous Practice of Prayer

By JAMES SPENCER, PHD

Let us cry mightily to God that we may have a double portion of the Holy Spirit, and that we may not rest satisfied with this worldly state of living, but let us, like Sampson, shake ourselves and come out from the world, that we have the power of God.

—DWIGHT MOODY

WHEN ONE READS D. L. Moody's work, it is difficult to avoid the topic of prayer. Perhaps more importantly, when one reads accounts of Moody's life by those who knew him well or witnessed his ministry, prayer is prominent. As R. A. Torrey notes, "D. L. Moody was a man who believed in the God who answered prayer, and not only believed in Him in a theoretical way but believed in Him in a practical way. He was a man who met every difficult that stood in his way—by prayer."[1] For Moody, prayer was not simply a means to get past the rough parts of life and ministry. Prayer was a quest to align life and ministry with God. It was an expression of his desire to follow God even when following God did not make sense.

As such, coming to prayer without a willingness to agree with God about our fallen condition would not do. Moody rightly recognized that prayer was not the Christian equivalent to rubbing a magic lantern. God is not a genie in a bottle beholden to grant those who pray three wishes (if not more!). Instead, Moody saw prayer as involving submission to God's will, which often demanded confession.

---

1. Torrey, *Why God Used D. L. Moody*, 15–16.

J. M. Hitchcock recalls a Sunday meeting Moody held at Farwell Hall in Chicago in which Mr. Moody had an altercation with some hecklers in the crowd noting,

> This night he was there, urging this one and that one to come in, and by and by there came along a couple of roughs. They were swaggering along with cigars in their mouths. They were very insolent to Mr. Moody. He could have stood that, but in the presence of ladies they used obscene and improper language, and that was something Mr. Moody had not the grace to endure. He slapped one of them, and some of us prevented a fight. I said, "Too bad, what will poor Moody do with the second meeting?" He went into that second meeting, and the first thing he did was to pray, with the tears rolling down his cheeks, and confessed his sin to God, and then he got up and told the audience what he had done, and how sorry he was, and how unchristian it was, and he led that meeting with all the success and all the results as if it had never happened. He was a greater man for overcoming that mistake than he would have been otherwise.[2]

Rather than ignore the incident, Moody sets aside his ego to pray. It is not a sanitized prayer that the meeting will go well or that God will bless the assembly, but a vulnerable, raw prayer of confession and repentance. Moody did not see prayer as a custom to be followed, but as a moment in God's presence that resists insincerity, falsehood, and self-justification. Moody's prayer was not designed to pacify the crowd who witnessed him losing his temper, but to admit the truth through confession of his own failings.

Prayer, in Moody's thought, is something we approach with an openness to the will of God and a readiness to follow where he leads. As Moody suggests in *Secret Power*,

> if we are full of pride and conceit, and ambition and self-seeking, and pleasure and the world, there is no room for the Spirit of God; and I believe many a man is praying to God to fill him when he is full already with something else. Before we pray that God would fill us, I believe we out to pray Him to empty us.[3]

It is in this emptying that prayer becomes a perilous practice because we must release who we think we are, what we consider best for us, and what we

2. Yale Divinity School Library, D. L. Moody Center Digital Archives (https://moodycenter.org/).

3. Moody, *Secret Power*, 31–32.

desire to have and be. We set ourselves aside to be re-formed by God as we submit ourselves to following where he leads. Prayer certainly comes with its own rewards (however unexpected), but it requires us to overcome the fear of loss we may feel as we set aside our own misdirected desires, agendas, and ambitions and allow our lives to be directed by God.

When Moody speaks of prayer, he speaks of an encounter with the God who seeks to transform us into something new. Because that "something new" is often beyond our capacity to understand or imagine (Eph 3:20; Rom 8:26), we will often experience it as unusual and uncomfortable. Yet, there is beauty to be found in the suffering that accompanies our experience of something new. In so much as prayer is a perilous practice, it requires us to remain open to the God whose desire is to see us "walk in newness of life" (Rom 6:4). As we do so, we should expect to struggle as we move from where we are to where God desires us to be. We should expect some pain as we continually put our flesh to death by accepting God's instruction.

Dwight Moody and Perilous Prayer

In his 1898 work titled *Men of the Bible,* Dwight Moody highlights the prayers of Abraham, Naaman, Nehemiah and many others. For Moody, prayer was not coincidental to what made these men "men of God." Rather, prayer was part of who they were. It was deeply embedded in their character like an engraving on a piece of metal. Prayer, in Moody's mind, is not only or primarily a matter of discipline, but a disposition toward the world so that "if any man has God's work lying deep in his heart he will have time to pray."[4]

Prayer was not a strategy for achieving some end or become a "great man" of some sort. Instead, prayer reflected a way of life that was surrendered to the will of God. It was a part of a life given over to God. Prayer, in this sense, is perilous because through prayer God changes us, moves us, and directs us to do as he wills. As Moody notes in his treatment of Nehemiah, "If you and I are to be blessed in this world, we must be willing to take any position into which God puts us. So, after Nehemiah had prayed a while, he began to pray God to send him, and that he might be the man to rebuild the walls of Jerusalem."[5] Prayer guides us toward the will of God and expresses our willingness "to take any position into which God puts us."

4. Moody, *Men of the Bible,* 60.

5. Moody, *Men of the Bible,* 59

Prayer, however, is perilous for another reason: it requires a willingness to embrace the truth of who we are. It requires confession. To confess our sins is to admit the truth of who we are, the ways in which we live according to the broken patterns of the world, and the times when we reject the wisdom of God to chart our own course. Prayer without a radical commitment to the truth is at best hindered and at worst pointless. As Moody notes, "If there is any sin in my hear that I am not willing to give up then I need not pray."[6]

For Dwight Moody, prayer also changed a person. It reoriented them within the world in noticeable ways. Those who pray have a new posture. They see with new eyes and hear with new ears. Referencing Neh 1 and 2, Moody connects Nehemiah's prayer with Nehemiah's appearance. When the king sees Nehemiah, he recognizes that Nehemiah looks sad even though Nehemiah "had not been sad in his presence" (Neh 2:1). Despite his respect for King Artaxerxes (2:3), Nehemiah cannot help but express his distress over "the city, the place of my fathers' graves" which "lies in ruins" whose "gates have been destroyed by fire" (2:3). This sadness is, according to Moody, conditioned by prayer because, "much prayer and fasting change the very countenance of a man."[7]

These three instances from Moody's work on Nehemiah illustrate his conviction that prayer is "perilous." It is not a practice that, when practiced faithfully, will leave one unchanged. In part, it will not leave us unchanged because "there has never been a prayer upon this sin-cursed earth that has been indicted by the Holy Spirit but was answered."[8] To put it differently, when we offer self-serving prayers, or prayers that are intended to fulfill our own misdirected desires, we should not anticipate that God will grant our requests. God is not in the business of giving us what we think we want. He is in the business of doing what is best for us. As Moody illustrates,

> In former years, I was very ambitious to get rich; I used to pray for one hundred thousand dollars; that was my aim, and I used to say, "God does not answer my prayer; He does not make me rich." But I had no warrant for such a prayer; yet a good many people pray in that way; they think that they pray, but they do not pray according

---

6. Moody, *Men of the Bible*, 55.

7. Moody, *Men of the Bible*, 59.

8. Moody, *Secret Power*, 65.

to the Scriptures. The Spirit of God has nothing to do with their prayers, and such prayers are not the product of His teaching.[9]

To pray in accordance with the Scriptures is, in a very real sense, to pray against our current state so that we may move to a future state in which we increasingly resemble our Lord and Savior Jesus Christ.

Moody's understanding of prayer as perilous is rooted in the notion that, as Christians, we submit ourselves to God's will. We no longer determine our own course but allow God to direct us and guide our paths. To do so demands that we set aside our own agendas, fears, and desires. This is, for Moody, beautifully illustrated in the prayer of Christ in the garden. When we pray, we anticipate that God will change us in some way. To pray is, in part, to seek to see God, the world, and ourselves differently so that we can live for him rather than for ourselves. As Moody puts it,

> What we need is to pray to God to lift us up out of this low, cold, formal state that we have been living in, that we may live in the atmosphere of God continually and that the Lord may lift upon us the light of his countenance, and that we may shine in this world, reflecting His grace and glory.[10]

When we "live in the atmosphere of God continually," we have little choice but to be transformed by his presence.

The Perilous Practice of Prayer in Today's World

Looking out on the landscape of the world today, it may seem as though humanity is flirting with what Nick Bostrom describes as the "vulnerable world hypothesis" (VWH). The VWH posits the potential "devastation of civilization" through the development of new technologies.[11] Such technologies are not limited to "machines and physical devices," but include 'scientific ideas, institutional designs, organizational techniques, ideologies, concepts, and memes."[12] Over the last decade we've watched a number of different "technologies," including, but not necessarily limited to, (1) social media and search monetization strategies, (2) conflicts between ideologies such as critical race theory and liberalism, and (3) fiscal mechanisms that influence

9. Moody, *Secret Power*, 65–66.

10. Moody, *Secret Power*, 81.

11. Bostrom, "Vulnerable World Hypothesis," 455–76.

12. Bostrom, "Vulnerable World Hypothesis," 458.

politics and policy, intersect to put the United States in a uniquely, though perhaps not unprecedented, position of vulnerability.

Thankfully, the fate of the body of Christ, even the body of Christ in the United States, is not tied to that of any nation. While Christians are right to concern ourselves with the "secondary theatre of witness" that is the political realm, to be a people who point a fallen world to Christ we must keep the "secondary theatre of witness" *secondary*.[13] God's people are secure God is with us. He is our security. Through prayer we come to experience God not as a more powerful version of ourselves or as a supplement to the political, technological, and socialcultural systems on which we depend, but as the *primary* and final authority in all things. Practiced faithfully, prayer demands that all things be made subject (or secondary) to Christ under whose feet God placed all things (Eph 1:22).

As a practice, prayer affords us the opportunity to demonstrate our conviction that God is unconstrained by the challenges of a broken world. Prayer does not seek an equal partner, but a Sovereign who does not share our limitations. To pray faithfully is to make ourselves vulnerable to seeing God, ourselves, and the world differently. To the extent that we acknowledge that God is infinitely more prominent than anything else we may love, fear, or desire, prayer puts our self-perception and our perception of the world at risk. It is in this sense that prayer is perilous. When done with a right heart, prayer opens us up to the often-painful process of setting ourselves aside so that God can use us.

While prayer, as a practice, *affords* us certain opportunities, it does not *guarantee* them. Our practice of prayer can easily become perverted. The "hypocrites" of Jesus's day prayed to inflate their own reputation (Matt 6:5). The "gentiles" approached their gods with "many words" thinking that they could exhaust their gods into given them what they wanted (Matt 6:7). We can build ourselves up through prayer and insulate ourselves from God (Luke 18:9–12) rather than admitting our sinfulness and baring our souls before the Lord (Luke 18:13).

Prayer, as a practice, can be manipulated. In *The Dangers of Christian Practice*, Winner highlights the manipulation of prayer through "corporate 'family' prayer (that is, prayer in which master or mistress led bondsmen and bondswomen to pray)."[14] She notes, "One way that slave owners put prayer to work in domestic management, then, was by teaching slaves

13. O'Donovan, *Ways of Judgment*, 5.

14. Winner, *Dangers of Christian Practice*, 958–59.

prayer that the slaves themselves might be expected to pray. These prayers reminded slaves of their status and gilded that reminder with the authority of Christianity."[15] By offering a catechism that sought to teach slaves prayers such as "O enable me to understand the greatness of my privileges, and to feel my obligations," or "I praise thee, that I have a master and mistress to provide food and clothing for me, and everything else I want. . . . Help me to honor my master and mistress—to be faithful in my performance of duty to them" slave owners reinforced the existing social relationship so that what was needed was a transformation of the mind of the slave rather than that of the masters.[16]

While we may be tempted to look at the New Testament instructions to slaves as a justification for such prayers (cf. Col 3:22–25; 1 Pet 2:18–19), we must keep in mind that there is a difference between the content of an individual's prayer that arises out of conviction for one's behavior before God and the use of prayer to attempt to shape a people into something less conformed to the image of Christ and more conformed to the needs and norms that serve those in charge.

To practice prayer faithfully requires us to approach our sovereign, wise, and benevolent Creator with a willingness to be conformed more closely to the image of Christ rather than with a desire for God to legitimize us and our view of the world. Prayer, even the prayer of other people, is not a means we use to get what we want, but to converse with God so as to bring about his kingdom and his righteousness. We do not pray at God, but in prayer we enter into dialogue with God on God's terms. In prayer, "a particular language is spoken: God's language."[17] Speaking in God's language reminds us that we are not speaking on our own terms but are conforming to God and his ways so that "the better a man learns to pray, the more deeply he finds that all his stammering is only an answer to God's speaking to him."[18]

Conclusion

In a brief set of sermon notes on the will of God, Dwight Moody jotted down these simple reflections, "What is the use of praying against the will of God?

15. Winner, *Dangers of Christian Practice*, 968.

16. Winner, *Dangers of Christian Practice*, 967–68.

17. Balthasar, *Prayer*, 14.

18. Balthasar, *Prayer*, 14.

Pray for my business most ungodly man for a partner. Promise to marry [an] ungodly man and then pray for peace." Prayer is not a means of manipulating God or of convincing him that our way is the right way. Instead, prayer is an act of submission to God's will even when it is not altogether clear exactly what God's will may be. If we approach prayer as if we were rubbing a genie's lamp to receive three wishes, we close ourselves off to the sort of perilous prayer that is part and parcel of Christian life.

God is no genie in a lamp. He doesn't grant our wishes. We should be thankful for that. Instead, as we pray, we trust that God will not leave us as we are or the world as it is. We pray for conformity and restoration. We pray in the hopes that God will change us into women and men increasingly capable of reflecting Christ in a darkened world because, as Dwight Moody once said, "In the place God has put us He expects us to shine, to be living witnesses, to be a bright and shining light. While we are here our work is to shine for Him."[19] As we engage in the perilous act of pray, may we be open to allowing God to change us despite our fears, ambitions, or desires. May we be vulnerable and prepared to trust the Potter to form the clay as only he can.

Bibliography

Balthasar, Hans Urs von. *Prayer*. San Francisco: Ignatius, 1986.

Bostrom, Nick. "The Vulnerable World Hypothesis." *Global Policy* 10 (2019) 455–76.

Moody, Dwight L. *Arrows and Anecdotes*. London: Christian Age Office, 1876.

———. *Secret Power*. Chicago: Revell, 1881.

———. *Men of the Bible*. Chicago: The Bible Institute Colportage Association, 1898.

O'Donovan, Oliver. *The Ways of Judgment*. Grand Rapids: Eerdmans, 2003.

Torrey, R. A. *Why God Used D. L. Moody*. New York: Revell, 1923.

Winner, Lauren. *The Dangers of Christian Practice*. New Haven: Yale University Press, 2018.

19. Moody, *Arrows and Anecdotes*, 134.

On Prayer and Perseverance

By LINDSEY HANKINS, PhD

*The world has no charms for me when I look up, but the trouble
with God's children is they do not look up enough.*

—DWIGHT MOODY

ANY THEOLOGIAN WORTH HER salt ought to, upon being tasked with an
essay on prayer, shiver. For one, even if we struggle to pray as often and as
earnestly as we'd like, few of us are truly ignorant of its power and scope.
According to Tertullian, God has set upon prayer nothing less than "every
power of doing good":

> Therefore, it knows only how to call back the souls of the de-
> parted from the journey of death itself, to strengthen the weak,
> to restore the sick, to cleanse the possessed, to open the doors
> of the prison, to loosen the chains of the innocent. The same
> prayer absolves sins, repels temptations, puts down persecutions,
> strengthens the weak-hearted, delights the high-minded, leads
> wanderers home, soothes the waves, confounds robbers, feeds
> the poor, governs the rich, lifts up the fallen, supports the un-
> steady, holds firm those who stand. Prayer is the buttress of faith,
> our armor and weaponry against the enemy that watches us from
> every side. So never let us set out unarmed—let us remember the
> station by day and the vigil by night.[1]

---

1. Tertullian, *Or.* 64. In what follows, selections from either Tertullian, Cyprian, or
Origen taken from this volume will be noted by the author's name, treatise title, SVP
(Saint Vladmir's Press), and page number. So, for example, the previous selection would
have read: Tertullian, *Or.* SVP, 64.

Just so, prayer is an intimidating topic on which to write. Even Origen, one of Christianity's most agile theologians, once said that "one of the most impossible things is to treat the whole subject of prayer accurately and reverently."[2] I tend to agree (hence, the shivering).

In an effort to avoid the impossible, then, this essay will not attempt a comprehensive account of prayer. Instead, I will begin with a broad constellation of ways the church has come to understand prayer before narrowing down to just one difficulty that reliably attends its practice: namely, why should we persevere in prayers that God seems to ignore? Intractable questions resist facile answers so, far from resolving tensions or dispensing with difficulties, I hope to offer, instead, a glimpse into deep reserves of inherited wisdom. The hope would be that, by doing so, otherwise dark passageways would be illuminated even if doing so does not, ultimately, nullify the challenge each of us will face in traversing them.

Let us begin, then, with some sage advice from Augustine. At the beginning of his *On the Trinity* he writes,

> Dear reader, whenever you are as certain about something as I am, go forward with me; whenever you hesitate, seek with me; wherever you discover that you have gone wrong, come back to me; or if I have gone wrong, call me back to you. In this way we will travel along the street of love together as we make our way toward him of whom it is said, 'Seek his face always.'[3]

The quote at the end is from Ps 105. This phrase—"seek his face always"—acts as a red thread, popping up noticeably at the beginning, middle, and close of the treatise. *On the Trinity* is one of the most elegant treatments we have on an especially tricky doctrine: how *should* we explain that the church believes in the Father, Son, and Holy Spirit, and yet we do not worship three gods? Augustine reminds us over and over again in his treatise to "seek His face always" in part because he wants to remind believers that knowing God is unlike knowing anything (anyone) else. Knowing God is first and foremost to be known *by* God—to be called home. This kind of knowledge requires loves wings because we cannot know a God we do not seek in love. Famously, Augustine tells us elsewhere: "You stir [us] to take pleasure in praising you, because you have made us for yourself, and

---

2. Origen, *Or.* SVP, 112.

3. Augustine, *Trin.* 1.5 (p. 68).

our heart is restless until it rests in you."[4] We must "seek His face always," says Augustine, because we are made to gaze upon it.

But what do we do when the seeking is difficult? Of the host of apparent and real tensions that exist in the biblical portrait of prayer, a central conflict is that we are called to continuous, persistent prayer (1 Thess 5:17; Luke 18:1) even though, Paul admits, we often hardly know how to pray in the first place (Rom 8:26). So goes one difficulty. In a similar vein, what do we do when God hides (or seems to hide) his face? What ought we do when he does not or delays in answering our prayers?

To wager a response to those difficulties we'll need to first offer a definition of prayer. God has already spoken to us in his law and his gospel, but in prayer he extends an invitation for us to join a lively and ongoing conversation that was first and foremost his. Once God's enemies, we have been brought near to God, into the very life of God, as both children and friends. Prayer, it turns out, is just what children and friends of God do *as* children and friends of God. According to Rom 8, those led by the Spirit are freed to call out by virtue of their adoption: *Abba, Father!* (vv. 14–16). And as the disciples learned at their last dinner together with Jesus, we are no longer slaves for we now know our Master's business (John 15:15). And since friends, as Thomas Aquinas reminds us, are those with whom we share our secrets,[5] prayer functions as one of the principal ways we live out that friendship with Jesus: in prayer we lay bare secrets God already knows in the hope that we may be transformed by the receiving of his. In this light, we can see how prayer is an invitation for children and friends to act as such.

Prayer is also a command, however. We are not told "if you pray" in Matt 6 but "when." Prayer is no pious adornment. It is not sweet; it is not quaint. This side of glory, prayer is a lifeline in raging storm. Karl Barth has a peculiar knack for detailing how the Christian life is largely an experiment in graced failure. Confronted by both law and gospel, we hardly know what to make of either. Just so, he tells us, the import of prayer can hardly be gainsaid:

> We find ourselves face to face with [God] when we are tormented
> by the imperfection of our obedience and the discontinuity of our

---

4. Augustine, *Conf.* 1 (p. 3).

5. Aquinas, *In Ioan., Prologue,* 11. All the works cited for Thomas Aquinas in this essay can be found at http://www.aquinas.cc, a searchable compendium with both Latin and English translations overseen by the Aquinas Institute.

faith. Because of God we are in distress. God alone is able to heal us of it. In order to ask him to do so, we pray.[6]

We are commanded to pray, then, because the ravishes of sin and the demands of Kingdom life require nothing less than perpetual divine intervention. They require an ongoing, life-giving conversation.

We are also commanded to pray because of Christ's example. Both his agonized plea at Gethsemane (*not my will but Thine*) and his teaching at the Mount (*your will be done*) testify to the radical emptyhandedness that constitutes Jesus Christ's incarnate life (Phil 2). Now if, as Barth tells us, Jesus Christ was from the very beginning . . . [the] elected man, then we have to say that God's eternal will has as its end the life of this man of prayer. This is the man who was in the beginning with God. This is the man who was marked and sought out by God's love. This is the man to whom and to the existence of whom the whole work of God applied as it was predetermined from all eternity.[7]

Accordingly, just as Christ fulfills what it means to be truly human in his life of perpetual prayer (i.e., by his perfect dependence on the Spirit to be led to the Father's will), so too by prayer do we become more truly human, for in prayer "confidence in self gives way before confidence in God."[8] We are commanded to pray, in other words, because in no small measure our very existence and flourishing depend on it.

This Christocentric, cosmic framing of prayer leads Barth elsewhere to name prayer as an act both humble and triumphant.[9] Prayer is necessarily humble because simply by *asking* for God's will to be done we admit that we cannot force it to be so. Indeed, by asking for *God's* will to be done we admit that we are not, in fact, gods ourselves. Prayer is necessarily triumphant, too, since it is a true participation in the ongoing work of God in creation. Prayer is how we collaborate with God for his good purposes.[10]

---

6. Barth, *Prayer*, 11.

7. Barth, *Church Dogmatics* II/2, §33 (p. 180).

8. Barth, *Church Dogmatics* II/2, §33 (p. 180).

9. Barth, *Prayer*, 21.

10. "Our participation in the work of God is the action that consists in giving our allegiance to this work. It is a great thing to preach, to believe, and to fulfill our small obedience to God's commandments. But in all these forms of obedience and faith it is prayer that puts us in rapport with God and permits us to live with him, and we on our side reply, 'Yes, Father, I wish to live with thee.' And then he says, 'Pray, call me; I am listening to you. I shall live and reign with you'" (Barth, *Prayer*, 20–21).

This immediate connection between prayer and providence follows a well-worn path. Thomas Aquinas, for instance, echoes many others when he claims that while our prayers contribute meaningfully to God's providential care, we ought not think that we are, somehow, filling in for some sort of divine lack. Instead, God has eternally ordained our prayers to play a true albeit dependent role, one of many intermediate causes "in order that the beauty of order may be preserved in the universe and also that he may communicate to creatures the dignity of causality."[11] In other words, when a Christian prays, she partners with the right order of God's loving care and is, in that act, reminded of her dignity as one invited and enabled to do so. Wonderfully, since right order is intrinsically beautiful,[12] when we fulfill our roles in prayer, Thomas thinks we also partner with God's ongoing creation of beauty. We are commanded to pray, in this light, because our lovely world awaits even more luminous strokes and God chooses not to be a solo artist.

So, to repeat one of our originating questions: why pray constantly? We can and must pray ceaselessly because we are told and invited to, because life is hard, choices are often confusing, and because God is our only sure hope. We pray constantly because we are tasked with contributing to God's symphonic creative project. We pray because, as Robert Jenson once put it, we simply are "praying animals."[13] We are made to "seek His face, always," and prayer is a principal way we do so.

For the moment, let's agree to agree on these points. Even so, how ought we make sense of Scripture's recommendation to pray constantly set alongside the admission from Paul that we hardly know how to pray? Luckily, this is one of those biblical tensions that turns out, in the end, to be no real tension at all. First, we do, in fact, know how to pray for none less than Jesus Christ himself has given us a perfect template for both the content and the ordering of our right desires in the Lord's Prayer (Matt 6:9–13; Luke 11:2–4, 11). Second, in his letter to the Romans, Paul does not merely set up a problem and let us stew in it. He does not, that is, tell us we do not know how to pray, period. Instead, immediately following the grim portrait painted in Rom 7, Paul tells us that sin has not—it

11. *ST* Iq.23a.8ad2; for another reference to the angelic contemplation of the beauty of divine order (*contemplantur pulchritudinem ordinis rerum a Deo derivatam*) (*STIq.108a.5ad4*).

12. As he puts it in his *Summa Contra Gentiles*: the order within the composite diversity of the universe is "the chief beauty in things" (3.71).

13. Jenson, "Praying Animal," 311–25.

cannot—conquer grace for "through Christ Jesus the law of the Spirit who gives life has set [us] free from the law of sin and death" (8:2). Rescued from servile fear, we have been named children of God, those newly enabled to call on their heavenly Father (8:14–17). Alongside the whole of creation, we groan for our true adoption to be made complete in glorious, eschatological expectation of our future resurrection (8:22–25). It is against this sweeping backdrop that Paul tells us that we do not know how to pray: caught between salvation and glory, still shedding strips of our burial garments, we may find ourselves unable to pray, ignorant of what our next steps ought be (or, perhaps, even of what we'd like them to be). Just then, Paul tells us, we must be reminded that the very Spirit of Christ our Intercessor is always already at work (8:26–27). In a very real sense, then, even when we cannot form the words to pray, still we pray ceaselessly to the extent that the very same Spirit who accompanied Christ from the manger to Golgotha and on to resurrected glory is forever at work in those being "conformed to the image of [the] Son" (8:29):

> What, then, shall we say in response to these things? If God is for us, who can be against us? .... No, in all these things we are more than conquerors through him who loved us. For I am convinced that neither death nor life, neither angels nor demons, neither the present nor the future, nor any powers, neither height nor depth, nor anything else in all creation, will be able to separate us from the love of God that is Christ Jesus our Lord. (Rom 8:31–32, 37–39)

Not even our ignorance and inability, says Paul, keeps us from offering up a constant prayer. Why? Because God has been praying for and through us before any of us ever stumbled upon the good sense to pray to and with him.

One startlingly important caveat to all this is, however, that Paul presumes that children of God will act like it. In other words, throughout Rom 8 Paul assumes that his audience is comprised of those who "live in accordance with the Spirit [and] have their minds set on what the Spirit desires" (8:5). As those made alive in Christ by the Spirit, "we have an obligation," says Paul, to live by that selfsame Spirit (8:12–13). Our minds are no longer "hostile to God," refusing to "submit to God's law" (8:7). Quite the opposite. We are precisely those invited *and* commanded to pray: *Thy will be done.* Cyprian puts it nicely:

> We should remember, therefore, dearest brothers, and realize that when we address God as our Father we should act as children of

> God, so that just as we have pleasure in having God as our Father,
> so he should have pleasure in us. Let us act as temples of God, so
> that it may appear that God dwells in us.[14]

Perhaps some of us modern readers may find it uncomfortable to tether our praying lives so closely with our moral or social lives, or to intimate that prayer does not regard God alone. And yet the biblical portrait makes it quite clear that our love for and obedience to God—our prayers to him, included—are deeply entangled with the lives of those around us. While there is a deep and abiding asymmetry, Christ's great love command is twofold:

> "Love the Lord your God with all your heart and with all your soul
> and with all your mind." This is the first and greatest command-
> ment. And the second is like it: "Love your neighbor as yourself."
> All the Law and Prophets hang on these two commandments."
> (Matt 22:37–40)

Indeed, time and again Jesus reminds us that the love we show and withhold to one another is precisely the love we show and withhold from him (Matt 25:31–46).

It ought to come as no surprise, then, that our prayers admit to a similarly duplex, albeit asymmetric, nature. At the very heart of the most perfect prayer, uttered and recommended by none other than Jesus Christ himself, is the petition which Augustine once labeled a "thunderous warning":[15] *forgive us* as *we forgive others*. For just as we ought not offer sacrifices to the Lord without first seeking reconciliation with our brother (Matt 5:23–24), so too, many saints before us have recognized that we cannot expect the Lord to hear our cries if we will not listen to those of our neighbor. Arguably, no one has put this better than Gregory of Nyssa:

> You ask to have debts forgiven; how can you strangle your debtor?
> You pray that [God] may blot out what is written against you, and
> you carefully preserve the acknowledgments of those who owe
> you something? You ask to have your debts cancelled, but you
> increase what you have lent by taking interest? Your debtor is in
> prison, while you are in church? He is in distress on account of
> his debts, but you think it right that your debt should be forgiven?

---

14. Cyprian, *On the Lord's Prayer*, SVP, 50.

15. Augustine, *Enchir.* 74.

Your prayer cannot be heard because the voice of him who suffers
is drowning it.[16]

Bitter pills, it turns out, are still sure medicine. As the fulcrum around which the entire Lord's Prayer pivots, Jesus Christ makes it clear that the reconciled are expected to reconcile.

Thus far I have followed through on the first of my promises (namely, a sweeping account of prayer, as such). The second remains. What sense can we make of divine delay? And when God does not seem to be listening, why on earth ought we persevere? To offer just one example of this difficulty in action, we can turn to what has to be one of the least preached upon texts of the Synoptics: Jesus's unsettling interaction with a concerned Canaanite mother in Matt 15. In this scene, Jesus disregards (v. 23), dismisses (v. 24), and even disparages (v.26) the woman before eventually heaping lavish praise upon her (v. 28): *Woman, you have great faith!* When Thomas Aquinas examined this passage, he claimed that it was "astonishing that the fount of goodness remained silent."[17] No doubt many of us would agree. Surely it is astonishing that Jesus ignores this desperate mother because this treatment does not fit a much-preferred portrait of God. Just before the Canaanite mother in Matthew's Gospel, for example, we have the story of Peter walking on water (Matt 14). Repeatedly that text reinforces the alacrity of God's response: "But Jesus *immediately* said to them" (v. 27); "*Immediately* Jesus reached out his hand and caught him" (v. 31). Pastors and preachers turn to this story time and time again for the clarity with which it displays the character of a God who is good and quick to come to our aid. Except, of course, when he isn't.

Think of it this way: to persevere in prayer—which we are everywhere told to do in Scripture[18]—requires that we do not have what we currently desire. I do not *desire* a hazelnut latte when I am drinking it on my porch early in the morning. At that point I am enjoying it. I desire that perfect mix of espresso and milk when it is not in my hand, when it

16. Gregory of Nyssa, *Lord's Prayer, the Beatitudes*, 80. He was not alone. From Tertullian: "For how can one approach the peace of God without peace, how seek the remission of debts whilst retaining them?" (*Or.* 11; SVP, 50). And Cyprian: "The Savior added and affixed a clear rule binding us by an assured condition and pledge, that just as we ask that our debts should be pardoned, following this we ourselves pardon those who are in debt to us" (*Or.*, SVP, 82).

17. *Super Matt.*, c.15, lect.2, n.1323.

18. To offer just a few examples, see: Jer 42:1–7; Luke 18:1–8; Mark 14:37–38; Col 4:2–4; 2 Cor 12:6–9.

is just out of reach, for whatever reason. By a similar logic, perseverance in prayer requires lack for, definitionally, we do not persevere—we do not strain towards—that which we have already obtained. The basic requirement for perseverance in prayer, then, simply is divine delay. Now it is one thing to ignore my desire for a triple-shot each and every morning. It is quite another to ignore my pleas that the cancer not come back, or that the memories would. Not one of us needs reminder that there is a world of difference between inconvenience and injustice. So why would a *good* God do this? Why ignore these pleas?

Before offering up a few good responses, we must first dispense with one very bad one. As will be news to absolutely no one, sometimes tragedy strikes. Sometimes horrendous things happen, even when we pray against them. And sometimes, when these horrendous things happen, some of us in the church say some version of "everything happens for a reason." Surely when believers say this, they intend it to be reassuring. The intent, likely, is to communicate that God is not absent and he has not lost control. This is true and good so far as it goes. Unfortunately, there is a vicious riptide to this platitude.

Years ago, Oprah vetted a book called *The Secret*. The book's quasi-Christian premise was basically that the energy or work or intention one puts out in the world is what one receives in return. So, if you want good things, the book argues, *intend* good things. If you want that job promotion, then put that intention out into the universe. If we extend this logic into our current register, the result is a sterile and egocentric form of prayer. It is truly terrible theology. Why? The notion that "one gets what one gives" only works for those whom the system already favors. It works for those who know tragedy or injustice or hate in theory, not in real life, on a Tuesday. This logic does not work for those choking under the boot of structures that were never meant to recognize them. It does not work for victims of assault, for example, who hear that, somehow, they got what they put out into the universe: that, somehow, *they asked for it*.

I do not know that god. Not everything happens for a reason because some things are simply and horribly wrong. Evil, in the end, is inexplicable. Children should not die in our wombs. They should not be in cages we built. They should not wash up on shores. God promises us in Revelation that he will damn—not explain or rationalize—death, injustice, and suffering of this kind. To remain true to its deposit of faith, to share truly good news, the church's message must be crystal clear: you did not ask for it. What has been done *to* you (what *you* have done!), these things are not the final word. We are braced on every side by grace upon grace (John 1:16) and it is grace, not sin, that gets the final word. So why doesn't God answer the prayers of those caught in horrendous evils? I couldn't begin to hazard an answer. And we must beware anyone who does for that is a wolf in sheep's clothing (whether they intend to be or not). Though it has been nailed to the cross with Christ, for the time being, the problem of evil really is a problem for those of us left groaning for the full, eschatological realization of Christ's triumph.

Not all unanswered prayers drill down to inexplicable occurrences of evil, however. In fact, there are a host of good reasons why God might delay or ignore our prayers. Perhaps the most common reason the church has given for God's silence is that sometimes we pray poorly: we pray for ugly things or, perhaps, for good things but just at the wrong time or in the wrong manner. Jesus once told us: "If you, then, though you are evil, know how to give good gifts to your children, how much more will your Father in heaven give good gifts to those who ask him!" (Matt 7:11). From this we can say that God does not answer some prayers—immediately or at all—because doing so would not be a good gift. Sometimes the hiccup is on the end of our asking: "You ask and you do not receive, because you ask amiss" (Jas 4:3).

Other times, God is up to something in his silence. This is precisely what Thomas Aquinas sees happening in the case of the Canaanite woman in Matt 15 we referenced earlier.[19] Thomas lists three reasons that Jesus ignores the mother. First, Jesus ignores this frantic mother for reasons that make narratival and theological sense. Christ ignores her, then, out of deference to his own recent instruction to the disciples to avoid gentiles like her (see Matt 10:5).

A second reason Thomas gives is that we are witnessing a test, albeit not one for her. By ignoring her—by delaying—Thomas says Jesus is giving his disciples a chance to fill the gap, to intercede on her behalf because no one is so good as to be exempt from needing another's aid in prayer. Our dependence rests principally on Christ our Lord, of course, but it is often mediated through his body. As Cyprian once had it, while we pray to the Father, in Christ and by the Spirit, we always do so from within our mother, the church.[20] It should be noted that in this particular story in Matthew's

---

19. See *Super Matt.*, c.15, lect.2, n.1319–50.

20. In praying to the Father as we ought, we also pray in and from our mother, the church, "for the name of Father and Son find their meaning in her" (Tertullian, *Or.*, SVP, 43).

gospel, the disciples fail fairly dramatically. Instead of filling the intercessory vacuum Christ creates, the disciples tell Jesus to send the annoying woman away. Even so, before any of us too quickly deride the disciples for their misstep, we would be well-advised to first take that pesky plank out of our eyes. Before condemning *them*, we ought to confess how quickly *we* get annoyed or prematurely dismiss those around us whose troubles do not resolve quickly enough. Unfortunately, too few of us pray on bruised knees. All to say, a second reason God sometimes delays is that we are, actually, the body of Christ and God expects us to act like it.

The third and final reason Thomas gives is one I want to end on. Thomas believes Christ ignores the woman to increase her devotion, sufficing to cite Hab 1:2–3 as his sole evidence: "How long O Lord will I cry but you do not listen? Or cry out 'Violence!' but you do not save? Why do you make me look at injustice? Why do you tolerate wrongdoing? Destruction and violence are before me; there is strife, and conflict abounds." This is Habakkuk's anguished cry. It is often ours, too, if we are honest. What Thomas does not cite but what I assume he expects his reader will recall, is God's incredible answer: "Look at the nations and watch—and be utterly amazed. For I am going to do something in your days that you would not believe, even if you were told" (1:5). Perhaps God delays, sometimes, because we simply cannot bear the good he has prepared for us now.

Remember how Augustine said our hearts are restless until they find their rest in God? Augustine also thinks our hearts need to be regularly broken open and re-made. In his words,

> The entire life of a good Christian is an exercise in holy desire. You do not see what you long for, but the very act of desiring prepares you, so that when God comes you may see and be utterly satisfied. Suppose you are going to fill some holder or container, and you know you will be given a large amount. Then you set about stretching that sack or wineskin or whatever it is. Why? Because you know the quantity you will have to put in it, and your eyes tell you there is not enough room. By stretching it, therefore, you increase the capacity of the sack, and this is how God deals with us. Simply by making us wait, God increases our desire, which in turn enlarges the capacity of our soul, making it able to receive what is to be given to us.[21]

---

21. Augustine, *Tract. ep. Jo.* 4.6 (cols. 2008–9).

According to Augustine, at least, the Christian life simply is an exercise of holy delay. We are seekers and wayfarers, pilgrims on our way. We are not yet where we long to be. Even more, we are not yet *who* we will be. Praise be to God.

So why does God delay *some*times? God delays sometimes because he is on a specific mission (where, for a time, gentiles will have to wait while he first deals with the Jews). He delays at other times because he was serious about us partnering with him in his providential care of creation, a task that is nothing less than beautiful to behold. Finally, God might delay because he will do anything—he has done *everything*—to bring his children, his friends, into cruciform likeness with his Son by the power of the Holy Spirit. Some delayed responses to prayer are aimed at teaching us that some things are simply worth the wait.

Recall that this essay opened with Origen's anxiety regarding prayer. It should be noted that, ultimately, he did end up writing an enormously influential treatise on the topic. Even so, it should also be noted that despite having accomplished his task with characteristic piety and erudition, he ends much as he began:

> I have struggled through my treatment of the question of prayer. . . . I do not doubt that, if you stretch forth for that which is before, and forget whatever is behind, and in the meantime pray for me, I shall obtain from God the giver a more extensive and more divine capacity with which to discuss these matters again in a manner more noble, more exalted, and more lucid. For the present, you will read this with indulgence.[22]

Prayer is a gift and a command. It is difficult and confusing. It is a lifeline. The best and brightest of our tradition have left in their wake a precious depository for which we can and should be eternally grateful. In the end, however, both its mysteries and its riches will reveal themselves only to its faithful practitioners, to those who seek the face of God with constancy and perseverance, always.

Bibliography

Aquinas, Thomas. *In Ioan., Prologue.* https://www.aquinas.cc/la/en/~Ioan.Pr.n11.4.
———. *Summa Contra Gentiles.* https://www.aquinas.cc/la/en/~SCG1.
———. *Summa Theologiae.* https://www.aquinas.cc/la/en/~ST.I.

22. Origen, *Or.,* SVP, 214.

———. *Super Matthaei*. https://www.aquinas.cc/la/en/~Matt.

Augustine. *Confessions*. Translated by Henry Chadwick. Oxford: Oxford University Press, 1991.

———. "Faith, Hope, and Charity." In *Ancient Christian Writers*, edited by Johannes Quasten and Jospeh C. Plumpe, translated by Louis A. Arand, 11–112. Washington, DC: The Catholic University of America, 1947.

———. *In epistuluam Johannis ad Parthos tractus decem* 4.6. In *Patrologiae Cursus Completus, Series Latina*, edited by Jacques-Paul Migne, vol. 35, cols. 2008–9. 221 vols. Paris: Excudebat Migne, 1844–92.

Barth, Karl. *Church Dogmatics* II/2. Edited by G. W. Bromiley and T. F. Torrance. Peabody, MA: Hendrickson, 2010.

———. *On the Trinity*. Translated by Edmund Hill. Hyde Park, NY: New City, 1991.

———. *Prayer: 50th Anniversary Edition*. Edited by Don E. Saliers. Louisville, KY: Westminster John Knox, 2002.

Cyprian. *On the Lord's Prayer*. In *Tertullian, Cyprian, Origen on the Lord's Prayer*, translated by Alistair Stewart-Sykes, 65–93. Crestwood, NY: St. Vladimir's, 2004.

Gregory of Nyssa. *The Lord's Prayer, the Beatitudes*. Translated by Hilda C. Graef, edited by Johannes Quasten and Joseph C. Plumpe. Ancient Christian Writers 18. Mahwah, NJ: Paulist, 1978.

Jenson, Robert W. "The Praying Animal." *Zygon* 18 (1983) 311–25.

Origen. *On Prayer*. In *Tertullian, Cyprian, Origen on the Lord's Prayer*, translated by Alistair Stewart-Sykes, 111–214. Crestwood, NY: St. Vladimir's, 2004.

Tertullian. *On the Lord's Prayer*. In *Tertullian, Cyprian, Origen on the Lord's Prayer*, translated by Alistair Stewart-Sykes, 41–64. Crestwood, NY: St. Vladimir's, 2004.

Lament: A Journey from Pain to Praise

By MAY YOUNG, PHD

We sometimes find that our prayers are answered right away while we are praying; at other times the answer is delayed. But especially when men pray for mercy, how quickly the answer comes!

—D. L. MOODY

Introduction

> "Come to me, all you who are weary and burdened, and I will give you rest" —Matt 11:28 (NIV)

In his exposition on this passage, D. L. Moody says the following:

> Now, there are a good many believers who think this text applies only to sinners. It is just the thing for them too. What do we see today? The Church, Christian people, all loaded down with cares and troubles. "Come unto me all ye that labor." All! I believe that includes the Christian whose heart is burdened with some great sorrow. The Lord wants you to come. Christ the Burden-Bearer. It says in another place, "Casting all your care upon Him, for He careth for you." We would have a victorious Church if we could get Christian people to realize that. But they have never made the discovery. They agree that Christ is the sin-bearer, but they do not realize that He is also the burden-bearer.[1]

Life is full of burdens and we can become quite weary. Jesus calls us to come and lay our burdens down before him so that we may find rest. Throughout the Psalms we find prayers that do this very thing. They are

---

1. Moody, *D. L. Moody Collection*, 112.

called Psalms of laments. However, the concept of a lament today is a bit of a misnomer. Many think of lament only as a way of unburdening or giving voice to our pain. While this is definitely an important part of the process, we are missing how lament is not an end in itself, but rather a journey to find healing and rest that can often result in praise. Many times the rest is experienced in the midst of waiting and surrender, resulting in greater hope. This process takes time and doesn't necessarily conform to our expectations, but it is through this willingness to honestly deal with our pain and suffering before God, that we can find healing and true rest. The journey of lament can usher us from pain to rest, resulting in praise and thanksgiving.

The following chapter will investigate how the overall structure of the book of Psalms, as well as the component parts and movement in individual laments, reflect the struggle that leads to praise. It will also examine how the process of lament can bring rest, greater hope and eventually gratitude expressed through praise. More specifically, Ps 13 will be evaluated as an example of this journey from lament to praise.

Structure of the Book of Psalms (Psalter)

God never promised an easy life. In fact, if we are honest, many would agree that life can be quite hard. We are all either coming out of a difficult time, in the midst of a difficult time or about to enter one. However, as Christians, we also see that these cycles of struggle eventually result in praise and thanksgiving. The book of Psalms, which has been recognized as the prayer and hymn book of God's people, reflects this reality. In his seminal work on the genre of the Psalms, Hermann Gunkel identified the following major categories: hymns (descriptive praise), songs of thanksgiving of the individual (declarative praise), laments of the people (communal laments), and laments of the individual.[2] While each of these major categories have specific elements that characterize them, many scholars, including Claus Westermann, recognize that the distinctions between the categories are not necessarily stark. "The boundary between the 'songs of thanksgiving of the individual' and the hymns is a fluid one. . . . The result is then that in the Psalter there are two dominant categories, the hymn (including the Psalms of thanks) and the lament."[3] In other words,

2. Gunkel, *Einleitung in die Psalmen*, 27, 30.

3. Westermann, *Praise and Lament*, 17–18.

what the Psalter or book of Psalms illustrates is that the human experience oscillates between deep anguish and profound joy.

Additionally, Westermann argues that structure of the book of Psalms depicts a trajectory from lament to greater hope and praise. He notes that literary arrangement of the Psalms shows a movement from lament to praise. The first half of the book of Psalms is dominated by laments, but larger groups of Psalms of praise or hymns appear only in the second half of the Psalter. "The first half of the Psalter is comprised predominately of Psalms of lament, the second predominately of Psalms of praise. . . . The Psalms of praise usually have the function of closing the collections, hence the doxologies at the end of the various books (e.g., Pss 41:13; 72:10; 89:52; 106:48; and 150)."[4] Patrick D. Miller Jr. rightly observes that this movement is by no means a simple linear direction. "There are hymns (Psalms of praise) in the earlier part, and there are laments toward the end of the Psalter (e.g., Ps 140–143). But the shift of emphasis is noticeable."[5]

Walter Brueggemann characterizes this movement in the Psalms as mirroring the life of faith for the people of Israel. Their experience moves back and forth from pain and anguish to surrender, joy, and celebration. These songs exhibit an authentic experience of life as it occurs. We live lives that are burdened with hurt, anxiety, loneliness, betrayal, as well as joy, celebration, and delight. More specifically, Brueggemann observes a movement in Ps 1 from moral duty and obedience to delight and praise in Ps 150. More specifically, this progression from willing duty to delight is only accomplished through the candid expression of lament. "In order to move from Psalm 1 at the beginning to Psalm 150 at the end, one must depart from the safe world of Psalm 1 and plunge into the middle of the Psalter where one will find a world of enraged suffering. In its laments Israel protests against the simplistic theological affirmations of Psalm 1."[6] Lament enables one to move from naïve obedience to the candor of true wrestling and questioning, resulting in greater hope, and even praise. He further argues that the key to this transition is coming to terms with God's *hesed*, or loyal love towards his covenant people. "Israel's struggle with God's *hesed* in suffering and hope, in lament and in hymn, in candor and in gratitude, and eventual acceptance of God's *hesed* as the premise of life permit Israel to make the move from obedience of Ps 1 to the doxology of

---

4. Westermann, *Praise and Lament*, 257.

5. Miller, *Interpreting the Psalms*, 67.

6. Brueggemann, *Psalms*, 197.

Psalm 150."[7] In other words, it is through the struggle of "experiencing" the failure of God's *hesed,* that one progresses from naïve obedience to surrender and greater hope in God.

Clearly, the overall structure of the Psalter reflects a movement from lament to praise, but this movement is not confined only to the general structure of the book. The structure of individual lament Psalms also portray a movement or journey that mirrors our human experience of struggle to greater hope and worship.

Structure of Lament Psalms

While the overall trajectory and structure of the Psalter is very instructive for understanding the journey from lament to praise, the individual laments also reflect, on a smaller scale, this progression and wrestling. To be sure, not all laments depict the complete trajectory from lament to praise; however, they all exhibit a dynamic development that moves beyond merely giving voice to pain and suffering. Westermann rightly observes that even though the Psalms of lament exhibit a rich diversity of expression, each one, without exception, exhibit an internal transition that can be recognized as being at least one step beyond simple lamentations. "There is not a single Psalm of lament that stops with lamentations. Lamentation has no meaning in and of itself. . . . What the lament is concerned with is not a description of one's own sufferings or with self-pity, but with the removal of the suffering itself."[8] Psalms of lament display a dynamic journey, not a static picture of self-pity. More recently, Frederico G. Villaneuva also recognized that even within laments themselves, there is a tension between lament and praise, and that the change in mood can move from lament to praise and back to lament, but the most typical pattern involves a transition from pain to praise.[9]

Additionally, John Goldingay argues that the dynamic movement in the individual laments exhibit more of a cyclical nature between lament and praise, rather than a linear progression, which is typical of Babylonian psalmody. More specifically, he would characterize it as a spiral, that when practiced in faith, exhibits greater growth. "The dynamic cycle of praise and prayer, prayer and praise might also be better seen as a spiral,

7. Brueggemann, *Psalms,* 202.

8. Westermann, *Praise and Lament,* 266.

9. Villaneueva, *Uncertainty of a Hearing.*

because of the fact that each journey round it leaves the believer a different person when he comes to the top of the circle from the person he was the last time he came this way."[10] As mentioned earlier, the movement in lament Psalms also depict a process from struggle that moves beyond mere lamentation. This journey is not an easy one, but it often leads to a greater sense of hope and even praise.

So how exactly does the process of lament help us to grow in hope that results in praise? I believe that we can learn from the general structural elements found in the lament Psalms themselves to address this question. Most scholars would agree with Westermann and Brueggemann that while there are definite distinctions between communal and individual laments, lament Psalms in general display a fixed structure with an unlimited number of variations. The following are some essential components that make up this structure: address, lamentation/petition/complaint, motivations, confession of trust/assurance of being heard, and vow of praise.[11] While these elements do not always appear in this order, nor do all the Psalms of lament contain every component listed, I believe that unpacking their significance can provide greater insight into how the process of lament moves us from merely unburdening our pain and suffering to praise and worship.

Address

Laments, especially individual laments, generally begin with an address to the Lord. Often times, the psalmist will refer to God's name (e.g., Pss 9:2; 54:1) or his character (e.g., righteousness and faithfulness Ps 4:1; 143:1). The importance of this component is that the psalmist is turning to God. This is a critical starting point because we need to recognize that lament is based on relationship. Brueggemann describes it as dialogical, indicating that prayers of lament are not just words spoken in a vacuum. They are spoken to God, the very one who can make a change.

D. L. Moody recognized the importance of this point as well. He says the following:

> Prayer is not a soliloquy, but a dialogue, not an introspection, but a looking toward the hills, whence cometh our help. There is a relief in unburdening the mind to a sympathetic friend, and faith feels

10. Goldingay, "Dynamic Cycle," 70.

11. Westermann, *Praise and Lament*, 265; Brueggemann, *Psalms*, 70. This list combines those listed by Westermann and Brueggemann.

> this abundantly; but there is more than this in prayer. When an obedient activity has gone to the full length of its line, and yet the needful thing is not reached, then the hand of God is trusted in to go beyond us, just as before it was relied upon to go with us.[12]

Today we are so prone to go to everyone, except the Lord. We would rather post about our frustrations on social media, or call up like-minded friends to unburden our thoughts, instead of coming to the Lord. In fact, many see prayer as a last resort. We only pray when we have exhausted all options. This is clearly reflected in the common statement, "I guess all we can do now is pray."

This first component of lament reminds us that we need to come before the Lord with our burdens, requests, and complaints. This also provides an important distinction between lament and merely grumbling or complaining. The wilderness generation in Exod 15–17 and Num 14–17 was condemned because they were grumbling and complaining against the leadership and against the LORD to each other. In other words, their complaints were not prayers. They were merely grumbling to themselves or to one another. They were not bringing this in prayer before the Lord. Complaint against God to others is condemned but bringing our complaints to the Lord is encouraged. Grumbling was just a way to express what they believe to be true about God. It was not dialogical, but just a means to air out grievances. "Whereas those rebels complained about God to each other, the psalmists (and Job) voice their laments directly to God. The latter indicates that they have not given up on God or abandoned hope that God would eventually answer their prayers."[13] By recognizing that laments are first and foremost an address to God, we are moving away from self-focused expressions of self-pity or frustration and turning to the one who can help us in our troubled and helpless state.

Lamentation/Petition/Complaint

This second component can be considered the actual "lament" section that leads to the "petition" of the psalmist. This can range from expressions of anguish, pain, hurt, anger, or even accusations against God or others. Generally, the lament can be a result of sickness (e.g., Ps 6:2), injustice

---

12. Moody, *Prevailing Prayer*, 103.

13. Longman, "From Weeping to Rejoicing," 219.

(e.g., Ps 73:4–10), personal sin (e.g., Ps 51:1–3), death (e.g., Ps 88:3–9), attacks from enemies (e.g., Ps 59:1–4), loneliness and abandonment (e.g., Ps 31:11–12), or shame and humiliation (e.g., Ps 69:19–20). This component highlights the honesty conveyed through the prayer. Often times, the psalmist expresses raw emotions of pain, disappointment, confusion, doubt, hatred, or even anger. There is no faking here. The psalmists are honest before the Lord. Moody also recognized the need for honesty in prayer: "Outspokenness is needful and powerful, both with God and man. We need to be honest and frank with ourselves."[14]

It is only when we are honest that we can truly deal with the issues that are burdening us down. Too many of us would rather sweep things under the rug or keep ourselves busy so that we don't have to face the ugliness and doubts that arise in our hearts. We don't want to confront our issues because it is often too painful. Life is not easy, but we don't have to handle it alone. We don't have to pretend or carry these burdens by ourselves. The psalmists have provided us examples for processing our doubts, pain, and struggles. When we face our issues with honesty before the Lord, we are allowing God to speak into the situation. We are no longer sitting in the echo chambers of our own mind or stuffing down our emotion. Instead, we are allowing the Lord to speak and look into the depths of our hearts. I liken this to the first steps toward physical healing. If we never address our physical health issues, we won't find the remedy that we need. We know from experience that our health issues won't just go away if we pretend they are not there. The first step is to go the physician so that he can examine us. We must expose ourselves and our pains to the doctor. This is not an easy process, and it can often be painful if we have left our wounds festering for some time. However, once we reveal our wounds or pains, we are one step closer to healing because the doctor can now prescribe the necessary treatment. Likewise, God is our Great Physician. When we come before him in full disclosure and honesty, no matter how ugly it is, we are expressing our desire for healing and wholeness.

Motivations

This next component often flows out of the lamentation, petition, and complaint. It is basically giving reasons for God to act or move towards action. These actions range from protection and salvation (e.g., Ps 86:1–4),

14. Moody, *Prevailing Prayer*, 33.

forgiving sins (e.g., Ps 25:11), healing sickness (e.g., Ps 6:2–4), to judging and dealing with enemies (e.g., Ps 7:6). Oftentimes it is an appeal to God's own reputation and name (e.g., Ps 25:11), God's past action or deliverance (e.g., Ps 22:4–5), the innocence of the psalmist (e.g., Ps 17:1–5), promise of praise (e.g., Ps 22:22), the helplessness of the psalmist (e.g., Ps 69:1), and the trust of the psalmist (e.g., Ps 57:1). This component of the lament Psalm bridges the requests with what the psalmist knows about God and his character. Many times the psalmist is reciting what he knows and heard to be true about God. This is an important part of the lament process because in our dialogue with God, we need to be reminded about whom we are talking to. As New Testament (NT) believers, it critical for us to know the God of Scripture. We are not approaching a God who doesn't care or who hasn't revealed himself to us. Just as God revealed himself as the Covenant God of Israel through the Law and the Prophets in the Old Testament, as NT believers we have the witness of all Scripture that tells us who God is. Because emotions can often be overwhelming, we need to refocus our minds on who God has revealed himself to be. Scripture can help ground us during our struggles and pain. Even though our experience seems contrary, reciting what we know to be true of God lifts our eyes to him. Moody also stresses the importance of Bible reading with prayer in the following:

> We have a great many prayer meetings, but there is something just as important as prayer, and that is that we read our Bibles, that we have Bible study and Bible lectures and Bible classes, so that we may get hold of the Word of God. When I pray, I talk to God, but when I read the Bible, God is talking to me; and it is really important that God should speak to me. . . . I believe we should know better how to pray if we knew our Bible better.[15]

When we know who God is, we can have confidence to appeal to him to act in accordance with his character and love. This helps move us from hopelessness to see that God is greater than our current circumstances.

Confession of Trust / Assurance of Being Heard

This next component is important for marking the shift from lament to hope. More specifically, it is the turning point from distress to trust in the psalmist. Many times this is indicated through the vocabulary of the

---

15. Moody, *D. L. Moody Collection*, 318.

psalmist. In Hebrew grammar, this is called a *waw* adversative, which is translated through the conjunction "but" or "now" (e.g., Ps 55:16, 23). "The *waw* adversative combined with the subject at the beginning of the clause indicates that here something else begins. . . . They indicate a transition from lamentation to another mode of speech, the confession of trust or the assurance of being heard."[16] It is important to note that the confession of trust and assurance of being heard are not synonymous. While they are distinct components, oftentimes there is not a clear boundary between assurance of being heard and confession of trust. For instance, the confession of trust may be the result of the assurance of being heard, and sometimes the psalmist mentions one while leaving out the other.

Understanding this shift has been investigated by many scholars.[17] And while there is no definitive answer, it is important for us to wrestle with this change from lament to praise. Perhaps the earliest and most prominent view comes from Joachim Begrich who proposed that these transitions indicate the coming intervention of God to the individual through an oracle of salvation by a prophet or priest (e.g., Pss 60:6–8; 81:6–10; and 109:7–9).[18] However, Westermann indicates that these oracles of salvation are hardly ever found in the Psalter, but occur frequently in the Prophetic books (e.g., Is 33:10–13). According to J. W. Wevers, the paucity of examples from the Psalms makes this view questionable. Instead, he proposes that the use of the divine name YHWH as a vocative along with an imperative verb indicates that there was power in the use of the name which gave the psalmist confidence (e.g., Ps 20:7).[19]

A recent article by Daniel J. Estes found Wevers's view to be too narrow in explaining the psychological transition. Instead, Estes argues that the transformation from pain into praise results from the psalmists' meditation on the works of God, his character and his word (e.g., Pss 77:12; 1:2; 9:8). "As the psalmists contemplate these theological truths, their view of their adversities is altered as the process of meditation causes them to perceive their experience through the lens of Yahweh's attributes and activity."[20]

---

16. Westermann, *Praise and Lament*, 71–72. Not all transitions are marked by the *vav* adversative (e.g., Ps 17:15).

17. See Villaneueva, *Uncertainty of a Hearing*, 2–27.

18. Begrich, "Das priesterliche Heilsorakel," 81–91.

19. Wevers, "Study in the Form Criticism," 80–96.

20. Estes, "Transformation of Pain into Praise," 162.

All of these proposals are helpful in identifying the transition exhibited in the lament Psalms, and perhaps the variety is necessary because of the plethora of human experiences. No single explanation can account for all the change in moods depicted in these lament Psalms. However, I do want to draw back our attention to the dialogical nature of lament Psalms because I believe that change from lament to hope comes because of who we are engaging with, namely God. As noted in the first component of lament Psalms, these prayers are addressed to God. When we are suffering, sometimes the ministry of presence is enough to move us into a more hopeful trajectory. Henri Nouwen notes, "[A]s we come to God with our hurts—honestly, not superficially—some-thing life changing can begin slowly to happen. We discover how God is the One who invites us to healing. We realize that any dance of celebration must weave both the sorrows and the blessings into a joyful step."[21] Perhaps it is just in being vulnerable and honest that we can experience an assurance of being heard and a confession of trust. I know that in my own life, times of lament, struggle and grief before God brought me to a place of surrender and release. Instead of holding on to the pains, questions, and doubts, I was able to lay them down in humble surrender before God. Without fail, it was through this process of honest struggle before God that I felt a spark of hope spring forth because I knew he had heard my prayers.

Vow of Praise

The final component is a vow of praise. This last element is closely associated with the previous assurance of being heard and a confession of trust. Often times, because the psalmist has felt the assurance of being heard or experienced deliverance, he is able to offer a vow or promise of praise (e.g., Pss 13:6; 56:12–13). According to Westermann, this is a constant component of lament and almost always appears at the end of the prayer. To be sure, not all psalms of lament have this component. Nevertheless, Westermann indicates that even though there are psalms that contain neither the assurance of being heard nor the vow of praise, they all exhibit a trajectory towards praise. "The cry to God is never one-dimensional, without tension. It is always somewhere in the middle between petition and praise. By nature it cannot be mere petition or lament but is always underway from supplication to praise."[22] This

21. Nouwen, *Turn My Mourning into Dancing*, 30.
22. Westermann, *Praise and Lament*, 75.

last component should remind us that even in our lament, God meets us and brings hope for a future time. Though we begin with weeping, God can transform our grief into dancing (e.g., Ps 30:11).

Walking through these different components of lament Psalms, confirms that laments are more than just giving voice to pain and suffering. Instead, what we see is a journey from honest confession and struggle before God which leads to alleviation of suffering, greater hope and oftentimes praise. It is important to note that in this process, lament and praise are juxtaposed to one another. It is not the forgetting of pain that moves us into praise. Instead, we see pain and suffering alongside gratitude and praise. Henri Nouwen rightly observes that our tendency is to divide our past into good things that merit gratitude and painful things that we would rather forget is just another way of avoiding our suffering. Instead, we need to recognize that all of life is to be received thankfully: "True gratitude embraces all of life: the good and the bad, the joyful and the painful, the holy and the not-so-holy. We do this because we become aware of God's life, God's presence in the middle of all that happens."[23]

An Example: Ps 13

Now that we have discussed the major components of lament psalms, let us examine these components in Ps 13:

> How long, LORD? Will you forget me forever?
>> How long will you hide your face from me?
> How long must I wrestle with my thoughts
>> and day after day have sorrow in my heart?
>> How long will my enemy triumph over me?
> Look on me and answer, LORD my God.
>> Give light to my eyes, or I will sleep in death,
> and my enemy will say, "I have overcome him,"
>> and my foes will rejoice when I fall.
> But I trust in your unfailing love;
>> my heart rejoices in your salvation.
> I will sing the LORD's praise,
>> for he has been good to me" (Ps 13:1–6)

23. Nouwen, *Turn My Mourning into Dancing*, 30.

Address (v. 1): This psalm begins with a series of lamenting questions directed at Yahweh, which continues into the next verse. It is clear from the beginning that the psalmist is directing his prayer to the one whom he believes can answer him.

Lamentation/Petition/Complaint (vv. 1–3): Here we see the complaint and lamentation expressed through questions about God's absence, as well as his struggle with sorrow that is most likely brought about through his enemies. These cries are honest and direct. Even though the psalmist feels like God has hidden his face, he will still engage God in faith. Instead of turning away from God because he senses his absence, he presses into God more directly. The complaint and lamentation then moves into a petition in verse 3 for God to take notice and bring deliverance from his sickness and grief. When the eyes were enlightened, it signifies health (e.g., Deut 34:7); therefore, the psalmist is imploring for God to heal him. There is a sense of boldness in this lament. You can sense the psalmist's desperation to engage God in the midst of his pain and suffering.

Motivations (vv. 3b–4): The psalmist appeals to God's compassion and justice. The enemy in verse 4 is most likely referring to death, which is mentioned in verse 3b. In other words, he is asking God to save him lest death has the final word. Additionally, the foes, which is in plural form, is most likely referring to his physical enemies who would taunt him if God doesn't deliver.

Confession of trust / Assurance of being heard (v. 5): The shift from verse 4 to verse 5 displays an obvious shift from lament to hope. While the text doesn't give specific reasons for this, we can see the shift indicated through the *waw* adversative combined with the subject "But I" at the beginning of verse 5. Clearly, the psalmist is making a confession of trust. He is trusting in God's *hesed* or unfailing love and is therefore confident in his salvation for the future. Hope and confidence are expressed through these statements in v. 5.

Vow of praise (v. 6): The psalmist now ends with a vow of praise to the Lord for his goodness. What began with lamentation and complaint has progressed to a vow of praise. As you can see, this psalm of lament clearly exhibits the psalmist's journey from struggle to praise and worship.

Conclusion

As D. L. Moody reminds us, Christ is our burden-bearer. The book of Psalms and individual lament psalms demonstrate that coming before the Lord with our laments and pain is not merely an honest display of doubt, struggles and agony. Instead, we find in the structure of the Psalter and in lament psalms themselves, a journey that moves from pain to praise. However, this process is not always straightforward. God doesn't work on our timetable, and oftentimes it requires patience, but God desires for us to come to him and to lay our burdens down. The following exhortation from D. L. Moody is a fitting conclusion for this chapter:

> We sometimes find that our prayers are answered right away while we are praying; at other times the answer is delayed. But especially when men pray for mercy, how quickly the answer comes! Look at Paul when he cried, "O Lord, what wilt Thou have me to do?" The answer came at once. Then the publican who went up to the temple to pray—he got an immediate answer. The thief on the cross prayed, "Lord, remember me when Thou comest into Thy Kingdom!" and the answer came immediately—then and there. There are many cases of a similar kind in the Bible, but there are also others who prayed long and often. The Lord delights in hearing His children make their requests known unto Him—telling their troubles all out to Him; and then we should wait for His time.[24]

Bibliography

Begrich, Joachim. "Das priesterliche Heilsorakel." *ZAW* 52 (1934) 81–91.

Brueggemann, Walter. *The Psalms and the Life of Faith*. Minneapolis: Fortress, 1995.

Estes, Daniel J. "The Transformation of Pain into Praise: In the Individual Lament Pslams." In *The Psalms: Language for All Seasons of the Soul*, edited by David M. Howard Jr. and Andrew J. Schmutzer, 151–64. Chicago: Moody, 2013.

Goldingay, John. "The Dynamic Cycle of Praise and Prayer in the Psalms." In *The Poetic Books: A Sheffield Reader*, edited by David J. A. Clines, 67–72. England: Sheffield Academic Press, 1997.

Gunkel, Hermann. *Einleitung in die Psalmen*. Göttingen: HATII, 1933.

Longman, Tremper, III. "From Weeping to Rejoicing: Psalm 150 as the Conclusion to the Psalter." In *The Psalms: Language for All Seasons of the Soul*, edited by David M. Howard Jr. and Andrew J. Schmutzer, 219–28. Chicago: Moody, 2013.

Miller, Patrick D., Jr. *Interpreting the Psalms*. Philadelphia: Fortress, 1986.

Moody, D. L. *The D. L. Moody Collection*. Karpathos Collections. N.p.: Karpathos, 2015.

24. Moody, *Prevailing Prayer*, 112.

———. *Prevailing Prayer*. Abbotsford: Aneko, 2018.

Nouwen, Henri. *Turn My Mourning into Dancing: Finding Hope in Hard Times*. Nashville: Nelson, 2001.

Villaneueva, Frederico G. *The Uncertainty of a Hearing: A Study of Sudden Change of Mood in the Psalms of Lament*. Supplements to Vetus Testamentum 121. Leiden: Brill, 2008.

Westermann, Claus. *Praise and Lament in the Psalms*. Atlanta: John Knox, 1981.

Wevers, John William. "A Study in the Form Criticism of Individual Complaint Psalms." *Vestus Testamentum* 6 (1956) 80–96.

Lament as Prayer

By BRYAN C. BABCOCK, PhD

I'd rather be able to pray than to be a great preacher; Jesus Christ never taught his disciples how to preach, but only how to pray.

—DWIGHT L. MOODY

Introduction

"HOW CAN A GOOD God allow this kind of tragedy?"

I work with a faith-based international disaster relief organization and have heard this question many times. I heard this question from a Christian family who had their house bombed in Syria by the Syrian National Army. They walked four days from Northern Syria to Iraqi Kurdistan—still in their pajamas. They had not eaten and had to pay their life savings as bribes to get out of the country. The family would rock back and forth in a small tent repeating, "How can God allow this to happen to us!"

People in Honduras in 2020 experienced two major hurricanes. Families lost their homes and entire village due to vast flooding—all during a global pandemic. They were in shock, hungry, and without shelter. You could hear people saying, "How can God allow this to happen to us?"

In 2021, a few months ago, I went to Ethiopia in the Tigray region where a civil war left hundreds of thousands of people displaced from their homes. They walked for days to flee the conflict, finding refuge in the high desert city of Shire (pronounced Sheer-ā). I use "refuge" loosely as people found that the only places to stay were unfinished concrete structures—without shelter, limited water, limited food, and no bathrooms. When I arrived, people were having to go to the bathroom in an open field. The amount of refuse was so large that the smell was overwhelming. Worse, urine and the water supply were beginning to mix and pool—increasing the likelihood of disease. I had never seen such inhumane conditions. People asked, "How could God allow this to happen to us!"

Tragedy is hard and painful. We ask how a loving, gracious, and merciful God can allow tragedy and suffering. Many of us reading this essay have not been impacted by war or natural disasters. However, each of us has likely experienced some form of personal devastation. When afflicted with a disease, the breakup of a marriage, the loss of a child, natural disaster, or financial calamity, how should we respond? In our pain, what do we say to God?

C. S. Lewis writes, "God whispers to us in our pleasures, speaks to us in our conscience, but shouts in our pain, it is his megaphone to rouse a deaf world."[1] Perhaps this is true, but how can we hear during the deafening volume of our pain?

When Jesus faced this moment of pain, what did he ask? Jesus quoted Ps 22 saying, "My God, My God, why have you forsaken me?" (Matt 27:46). In Ps 22, David first wrote those words. David goes on, "Why are you so far from saving me, so far from my cries of anguish? My God, I cry out by day, but you do not answer, by night, but I find no rest" (Ps 22:1–2).

Have you been there? Have you truly wondered how God could allow [insert your tragedy] to happen to you or your family? Mark Vroegop in *Dark Clouds Deep Mercy* shares that the earliest experience of a newborn child is to cry. Leaving the safety and security of the womb and being thrust into a painful existence is hard. The response is with tears and crying—loud and with all our being. To *cry* is a human response to suffering and tragedy.

Lament can be defined as a loud cry, a howl, and a passionate expression of grief. However, it is so much more. Lament gives an honest voice to the emotions that believers feel because of tragedy. According to Michael Card, lament asks two questions:

1) Where are you God? And,

2) God, if you love me why is this happening?[2]

Lament is a prayer in pain that leads to trust. Going back to Psalm 22, David starts with "My God, My God." Even in his pain and suffering, David knows that God is real! David is not praying to "a God"; he is reaching out to "*My God*"! Nicholas Wolterstorff writes, "I shall look at

1. Lewis, *Problem of Pain*, 93.
2. Card, *Sacred Sorrow*, 17.

the world through tears. Perhaps I shall see things that dry-eyed I could not see."[3] Through this essay, we will look through our tears and strive to embrace lament as prayer with the goal of trusting God. To begin our exploration of lament as prayer in times of tragedy and suffering, I would start with the idea first proposed by Vroegop that "to cry is human, but to lament is Christian."[4]

To Cry Is Human, to Lament Is Christian

Lament begins in crisis and ends in praise. It is quite simple for us to understand the former as our world is full of pain and suffering. However, I have often been confused at the notion of the psalmist who in a few short lines is able to transition from being in the pits of despair to praising God. It felt, somehow, simplistic and lacking in genuine human character.

As we move through this essay, I hope to orient you to the power of lament as prayer during times of suffering. Before we delve into the components of a lament let's first explore the central feature of a lament—God.

Vroegop writes that "belief in God's mercy, redemption, and sovereignty create lament. Without hope in God's deliverance and the conviction that he is all-powerful, there would be no reason to lament when pain invaded our lives."[5] Trust that God has the power to act and trust that God's character will have him act are essential to Christianity. If the psalmist had already decided that God was either unable or unwilling to respond, then there is no reason to write! We might as well just cry.

Therefore, as Christians, we can confirm that the world is broken, God is all powerful, and he will be faithful. It is this belief that allows lament to stand in the gap between pain and promise.

Classic Structure of Lament

To better understand lament as it is used in the Psalms, and more broadly throughout the Bible, it is important to explore the construction, use, and context of lament. A lament psalm (and laments in most parts of the Bible) are defined by five distinct sections: 1) an invocation or address to

3. Wolterstorff, *Lament for a Son*, loc. 127 of 562.

4. Vroegop, *Dark Clouds, Deep Mercy*, 26.

5. Vroegop, *Dark Clouds, Deep Mercy*, 26.

God, 2) a description of the complaint, 3) a request for help, 4) an expression of trust based upon God's character and past actions, and 5) change of perspective—praising of God.[6]

Invocation to God

As a brief example, let's explore Ps 10. The psalm begins like most laments with an address to God. This brief section includes agonizing questions. The author reveals a sense of isolation and distance from the Lord.

> Why, Lord, do you stand far off?
>
> Why do you hide yourself in times of trouble? (Ps 10:1)

The author is experiencing suffering and God is nowhere to be found. God is not paying attention. Even more, the psalmist notes that God is actively hiding himself during times of suffering. The very fact that people have to cry out verifies that God can, at times, seem distant—standing out of site and hiding from us during times of trouble.[7]

Complaint

The second section is a description of the complaint and current situation. Ps 10 continues in verses 2–11:

> In his arrogance the wicked man hunts down the weak,
>
> who are caught in the schemes he devises;
>
> He boasts about the cravings of his heart;
>
> he blesses the greedy and reviles the Lord. . . .
>
> His ways are always prosperous;
>
> your laws are rejected by him;
>
> he sneers at all his enemies.
>
> He says to himself, "Nothing will ever shake me."
>
> He swears, "No one will ever do me harm." . . .
>
> He says to himself, "God will never notice;
>
> he covers his face and never sees." (Ps 10:2–11)

6. Different scholars find between four and seven sections of a lament psalm. In this essay we are following Westermann, *Praise and Lament*, 52.

7. Goldingay, *Psalms*, 185.

The psalmist writes about an evil person who is prospering at the expense of the community. Evil at any time is horrible. However, verse 11 tells us that the evildoer is part of the covenantal community. Even worse, they openly reject the godly way of life in favor of freedom and power.[8] The psalmist's prayer is an honest assessment of where God has failed to act and allowed evil to prosper.

Asking God to Act

The third section asks God to act, and act now! Verses 12 and 13 petition God for help:

> Arise, Lord! Lift up your hand, O God.
>> Do not forget the helpless.
>> Why does the wicked man revile God?
>> Why does he say to himself,
>> "He won't call me to account"? (Ps 10:12–13)

These concise verses answer the sprawling complaint with three primary requests. First, the psalmist prays that God will not forget his people. That he will see his people and act. Second, that God will lift his hand of power and act to break the control of the wicked. Third, that God will hold those evildoers accountable for their actions.

Remember God's Character and Prior Action

Turning to the fourth section, we find the pivot point of the prayer. We now find a "but" clause turning us from the past to the future.[9] Everything that the psalmist feels in the current situation is true. However, these things are *also* true. This section speaks to God's character or prior historic actions. Psalm 10:14–15 read,

> *But* you, God, see the trouble of the afflicted;
>> you consider their grief and take it in hand.

---

8. VanGemeren, *Psalms*, 155.

9. Westermann, *Praise and Lament*, 71–75. Westermann provides an excellent discussion of the *waw* adversive. This chapter essay that the hinge of a lament is found in the *waw adversive* as a statement of trust leading to praise. The *waw* adversive contrasts what has come before with what is about to happen.

> The victims commit themselves to you;
>> you are the helper of the fatherless;
> Break the arm of the wicked man;
>> call the evildoer to account for his wickedness
>> that would not otherwise be found out. (Ps 10:14–15)

Walter Brueggemann notes that this is the section of the psalm where the rhetoric changes from "I" to "You." God now becomes the center of the discussion. In addition, the psalm engages in concrete remembering which shifts our attention onto God and off the hopelessness of self.[10]

Based upon God's character, the psalmist knows that God does see those who are afflicted. In fact, God has helped the fatherless in the past and has broken the arm of men who have acted wickedly in the past. Therefore, God will bring the wicked to account for their actions as he has in the past. The situation has not changed . . . yet. However, the psalmist has confidence that things will change and God will act.

Confidence That Our Situation Will Improve

The psalm concludes with praise and confidence that things will improve. The psalmist writes:

> The Lord is King for ever and ever;
>> the nations will perish from his land.
> You, Lord, hear the desire of the afflicted;
>> you encourage them, and you listen to their cry,
> defending the fatherless and the oppressed,
>> so that mere earthly mortals
> will never again strike terror. (Ps 10:16–18)

One in three of the psalms is a lament. Considering the prominence of laments in the Psalms, it is surprising how little time we study lament in our church sermons and how few worship songs include lament. Perhaps our Western cultural bias to keep our pain hidden and only discuss the positives in our lives is to blame. Or is it possible that our unfamiliarity with lament is a byproduct of a subtle misunderstanding of Christian suffering?

10. Brueggemann, *Israel's Praise*, 138.

Vroegop writes that "laments are in the Bible for a reason. Understanding a song of pain is vital to the life of God's people. There's something uniquely Christian about lament, something redemptive, and something full of faith."[11] Armed with a basic understanding of the structure of lament, we now turn to explore how to utilize a prayer of lament in our personal pain and suffering.

Lament as a Personal Prayer

I frequently hear two questions while working with people during disasters: 1) *How* can a good God allow this kind of suffering? 2) *Where* is God during times of suffering?

These are not new questions, and the lament psalms give us some excellent examples. Let us start by exploring Ps 88. The psalmist asks:

> But I cry to you for help, Lord;
>
> > in the morning my prayer comes before you.
>
> Why, Lord, do you reject me
>
> > and hide your face from me? (Ps 88:13–14)

The psalmist is not crying to the universe or to a neighbor. No, the writer is aware that God exists, and the prayer is focused on the LORD. Therefore, when we are suffering we should start with an awareness of God. Even if that awareness is acknowledging that God does not seem present with us.

The psalm continues . . .

> From my youth I have suffered and been close to death;
>
> > I have borne your terrors and am in despair.
>
> Your wrath has swept over me;
>
> > your terrors have destroyed me.
>
> All day long they surround me like a flood;
>
> > they have completely engulfed me.
>
> You have taken from me friend and neighbor—
>
> > darkness is my closest friend. (Ps 88:15–18)

11. Vroegop, *Dark Clouds*, 30.

Be Honest with God

It is essential in a prayerful lament to be honest with God. The psalmist is taking a frank look at their current situation. They are in touch with their emotions and are being candid with God. In church we are taught to praise God in all things. Our hymns and worship are positive and uplifting . . . but life is not always joyous.

The Billy Graham Evangelistic Association reports that as many as 90 percent of people affected during a disaster were already experiencing severe suffering *before* the disaster. Think about that: it means that most people who surround us every day are likely experiencing something traumatic in their lives. This could be financial issues, marital problems, substance abuse, grief, and loss.[12]

Yet, in church most of our preaching and worship is directed towards the notion that everything should be OK if we are right with God. *Wrong!* Things are not always fine even if we are right with God.

Many Christian are afraid or ashamed to be honest with God and this creates a gulf between the expectation we are taught in church and the reality of our lives. Many of us feel that if things are falling apart around us then it must be our fault and God does not want to hear from us. The result is that we stop talking to God about our pain and suffering. All too often this can lead people into a spiritual wilderness and an inability to communicate with the Lord.

This is exactly the opposite of what we need to be doing. We need to reach out to God during times of suffering and be sincere about what we are feeling.

If we are going to be honest with God, that includes being angry with God. Going back through the verses above, the psalmist cries out that God has brought (or at least allowed) this suffering. God's wrath has swept over him and separated him from both health and relationships. His friends are gone, and darkness is his only friend. The psalmist is angry that God has allowed both health and relationships to suffer.

In 2000, I had the knock on the door that every parent fears: the loss of a child. You are never prepared for this type of loss. The doorbell rings and on the other side is a police officer and a chaplain. Instantly you know something terrible has happened, yet time freezes and you cannot move. In my case it was an accident where my fifteen-year-old son was struck and killed

---

12. From Graham, "Sharing Hope in Crisis."

by a car. I knew that God existed. However, I also knew that I no longer liked a God who could allow this to happen. How could the God we read about in the Bible allow parents to lose a son! I was angry—angry at God.

We need to recognize that God is all knowing, all powerful, and supreme. However, we do not always have to understand his will—nor do we have to be happy about it. If you are angry, tell God how you were wronged and why you are angry with him. Do not keep that bottled up and pretend everything is alright.[13]

List Your Complaints

Next, list your complaints, questions, and frustrations. Try to understand why you feel the way you do. As you pray, ask God the questions of your heart and share your frustrations.

Does this idea make you a bit anxious? If so, you are not alone. We are taught to be quiet and to know that God is God. Having feelings means that we are not being *good* Christians. But it is biblical to share your questions with God through a prayer of lament.

In fact:[14]

Paul experienced many painful emotions, including . . .

- Anguish of heart—2 Cor 2:4
- Anxiety—Phil 2:28
- Great distress—2 Cor 2:4
- Fear—2 Cor 11:3; 7:5
- Grief—2 Cor 12:21

Jesus: As he anticipated being crucified, Jesus felt:

- Deeply distressed and troubled—Mark 26:38
- Overwhelmed with sorrow—Matt 26:38
- Distressed—Luke 12:50
- Troubled in heart and in spirit—John 12:25

13. Thanks to John Freyler who equates this process to the twelves steps towards forgiveness as outlined by Anderson, *Victory over the Darkness*.

14. My thanks again to John Freyler from Samaritan's Purse for providing this list.

David: David's emotional responses to suffering included:

- Agony—Ps 6:2
- Anguish—Ps 6:3
- Distress—Ps 4:1
- Fear—Ps 34:4
- Grief—Ps 31:9
- Groaning—Ps 22:1
- Sorrow—Ps 6:7
- Weeping—Ps 6:6

Here are a few examples of questions from prayers of lament in the Psalms:

> How long, O LORD? Will you forget me forever?
>
> How Long will you hide your face from me? (Ps 13:1)
>
> O LORD, why do you cast my soul away? (Ps 88:14)
>
> In his arrogance the wicked man hunts down the weak,
>
> who are caught in the schemes he devises. (Ps 10:2)
>
> "Will the Lord reject forever?
>
> Will he never show his favor again?
>
> Has his unfailing love vanished forever?
>
> Has his promise failed for all time?
>
> Has God forgotten to be merciful?
>
> Has he in anger withheld his compassion?" (Ps 77:7–9)

As you read through the lament psalms you will begin to see that the psalmist is troubled that God is acting in a way contrary to his character. God is not being God-like!

Vroegop writes, "If you are comfortable with this, then you probably don't understand what is said here. The psalmist is deeply struggling, and not just with his pain; he's struggling with God. Injustice is one thing, but God's lack of intervention is a deeper pain—one that creates complaint."[15]

From our current position God is not acting the way he should . . . we are alone, hurting, abused, and in pain. Tell God these things! Let God

---

15. Vroegop, *Dark Clouds*, 46.

know your questions and complaints. Lament psalms give us encouragement to present our struggles, even if those struggles are with God himself. Complaint gives a voice to the hard questions!

Stay True to Scripture

To this point in the process, I have asked you to look inside yourself and communicate with God about how you feel. Now it is time to look to scripture and pray a lament biblically. The words may or may not be on your tongue. Sometimes it is helpful to pray along with the words of lament found in the Psalms.[16] Other times it might be helpful to understand the limits for what the psalmist complains about. Here are a few examples:

> Awake, Lord! Why do you sleep?
> > Rouse yourself! Do not reject us forever.
> Why do you hide your face
> > and forget our misery and oppression? (Ps 44:23–24)
> How long, Lord God Almighty,
> > will your anger smolder
> > against the prayers of your people? (Ps 80:4)
> My God, my God, why have you forsaken me?
> > Why are you so far from saving me,
> > so far from my cries of anguish?
> My God, I cry out by day, but you do not answer,
> > by night, but I find no rest. (Ps 22:1–2)

When you do not have the words to pray, review the list of lament psalms at the end of this chapter and read through the verses. As you reflect on the words of the psalm, the Holy Spirit can work through you to find the right words for your prayer.

Don't Just Complain

We now turn to look forward, beyond our current suffering and complaint against God. I have tried to emphasize that many Christians skip the complaint when praying during times of suffering. As important as that is, it is also important not to get stuck in complaining. Vroegop summarizes this

16. Another excellent resource is https://traumahealinginstitute.org/.

point well when he writes, "[C]omplaint was never meant to be an end in itself. In other words, lament does not give you an excuse to wallow in your questions or frustrations. It is a means to another end. In the same way a surgeon's cut is meant to heal, so complaint is designed to move us along in our lament. You are not meant to linger in complaint. If you never move beyond complaint, lament loses its purpose and its power."[17]

Complaint is a starting point. We need to start by being honest with ourselves about our emotions and be honest with God about our struggles. This is true even when it is uncomfortable and awkward. Being honest with God about our labors sets the foundation for the next part of a prayer of lament—to remember who God is and what God has done.

Remember and Trust: Look for the But:

In the beginning of this chapter, I mentioned how lament psalms move from agony to praise. I have felt that the shift was both awkward and lacking in realism. This was because I missed the essential pivot in the psalms.

The key to lament is in the pivot between the two emotions. We start with our feelings of pain, sorrow, and feelings that God has forgotten our suffering. Then, we need to *act* and *remember* God. We need to remember how God has acted in the past. Remember what the Bible says about God's character. And remember how God has intervened for those who have suffered in the Bible.

> I will *remember* the deeds of the LORD; yes, I will *remember* your miracles of long ago. (Ps 77:11)

The pivot can be found in the Psalms following the words "but, yet, and for." Here are some examples:

> *Yet* you brought me out of the womb;
> you made me trust in you, even at my mother's breast.
> From birth I was cast on you;
> from my mother's womb you have been my God. (Ps 22:9–10)

Here the author remembers that God is, in fact, the creator and has cared for us since inception.

17. Vroegop, *Dark Clouds*, 53.

> *But* you, Lord, are a compassionate and gracious God,
>> slow to anger, abounding in love and faithfulness. (Ps 86:15)

The psalmist recalls God's character and that this instance in our life, while painful, will ultimately be addressed by God—as our current situation is not consistent with what we know about God.

> *But* you, Lord, are a shield around me,
>> . . . I lie down and sleep;
>> I wake again, because the Lord sustains me. (Ps 3:3–5)

As bad as our current situation is, God has sustained us thus far.

> *For* you are not a God who is pleased with wickedness;
>> with you, evil people are not welcome.
> The arrogant cannot stand in your presence.
> You hate all who do wrong;
> you destroy those who tell lies. (Ps 5:4–6)

We know that God's character will not allow this kind of wickedness to endure forever. We can trust in what we have read about God.

This pivot is essential to prayer during times of suffering. We need to express our honest emotions and pain with God. However, we need to not become stuck in those emotions. Our prayer must move beyond our current feelings and acknowledge God's character and prior actions in our life. Essentially, we can take inventory of what we know:

- We know that God has allowed us to live and has taken care of us thus far (Rom 8:37–39).

- We know that God can do all things and his purpose will come to pass (Job 42:2)

- We know that God is just and that injustice will eventually be judged (Eccl 3:17)

- We know that God created the world; the world fell and will ultimately be restored (Rev 21).

- We know that for those who love God, all things will work together for good, for those who are called according to his purpose (Rom 8:28).

- We know that God's love is eternal and his mercy never comes to an end (Lam 3:22)

- We know that if God is for us then nothing can triumph over us (Rom 8:31)
- We know that waiting is not a waste of time (Lam 3:25–27)
- We know that the final word is not yet spoken (Lam 3:31–32)
- God is always Good (Lam 3:33)

Armed with the truth that our current experience is not the end; the next step is to move forward in trust. We need to affirm in prayer that we trust that God will act in our current situation. A prayer of lament pivots on God's promises that lead us to trust.[18]

Keep in mind that nothing has changed in the author's current situation. They are still suffering, and their current circumstance is the same. The difference is *internal*. The psalmist has remembered that God is able to make a difference and the psalmist *chooses* to trust in God's character and prior actions. Our prayer of trust occurs even when the pain of our current suffering continues.

Rebekah Eklund says it well when she writes, "The prayer of lament rejoices in God's saving actions in the now and hopes urgently for God's saving actions in the future, the 'not yet' of the eschatological timeline. . . . It is shaped by the incongruities between what is and what should or might be; it is an instigator and sustainer of liminality. Those who lament stand on the boundary between the old age and the new and hope for things unseen."[19]

Lament prayer gives us a pathway to move from our current suffering to hope. The psalmist gives the following examples:

> But I trust in your unfailing love;
>> my heart rejoices in your salvation.
> I will sing the Lord's praise,
>> for he has been good to me. (Ps 13:5–6)
> As for me, I will always have hope;
>> I will praise you more and more.
> My mouth will tell of your righteous deeds,
>> of your saving acts all day long—
>> though I know not how to relate them all. (Ps 71:14–15)

18. Billings, *Rejoicing in Lament*, 38.

19. Eklund, "Lord, Teach Us to Grieve," 261.

But I trust in you, Lord;

I say, "You are my God." (Ps 31:14)

Remember that God is trustworthy, and take a step of faith, and pray that although our current circumstances are rotten, we trust that God will act. Below are a few trust statements from the Psalms that you might consider as you pray during times of suffering:

- There is no other like God—Ps 86

- Great is God's steadfast love—Ps 13, 52, 86

- God is merciful and gracious—Ps 86

- God is faithful—Ps 86

- God has helped and comforted me—Ps 86

- God is a shield about me—Ps 3

- I cried and God answered me in the past—Ps 3

- God sustained me through the night—Ps 3

- God protects me from my enemies—Ps 3

- I trust in God—Ps 31

- Source of my hope—Ps 71

- God is my helper—Ps 54

- My heart will rejoice in God's Salvation—Ps 13

- I will sing to the Lord—Ps 13

If you are stuck and cannot find words, Vroegop suggests a prayer that goes something like this:

> Lord, I'm weary and tired. I'm discouraged, and I don't know how I am going to do this again tomorrow. But I believe that I will never run out of your steadfast love, I'm trusting that you have enough grace for me for what I face. I'm going to sleep because I'm hoping in you.[20]

We should understand that trust is not the end to our situation. Trust will vary as we walk through the fires of suffering. Some days your trust will be a confident statement. Some days trust may be a simple and rehearsed statement. Some prayers might end in a song. Some might end by

20. Vroegop, *Dark Clouds*, 113.

reading a psalm like Ps 46:10—"Be still and know that I am God." Despite your emotional strength, build trust as you build a muscle—repetition and exercise. Armed with a new attitude, we are ready to ask God for assistance and trust that God will act.

Request with Confidence

Thus far we have discussed that a prayer of lament involves our sharing our emotions with God, being honest about our frustrations, remembering God's character, and making the decision to stand in faith. Now we turn the final step of lament: confidently ask God to act in accordance with his character.

Just as you were honest with God about your feelings, be honest about how you would like him to act. I think that in our pain we sometimes feel that God has already abandoned us and that asking for help is a waste of time, but that is not true.

At the depth of our sorrow, we reach out to God and ask boldly that God meet and protect us. The author of Hebrews writes, "Let us then approach God's throne of grace with confidence, so that we may receive mercy and find grace to help us in our time of need" (Heb 4:16).

The psalmist asks boldly for God to act. As you pray, think about what the Bible authors asked for when they were confronted with sorrow and pain. Here are a few examples:

- For God to Act—When we feel alone, we often need God to rise and act on our behalf. Psalm 3 is a good example when the psalmist writes: "Arise, Lord! Deliver me, my God! Strike all my enemies on the jaw; break the teeth of the wicked" (Ps 3:7). The exclamation points say it all. The writer is almost commanding God to rise. In fact, the idea of breaking his enemy's teeth shows that true anger and frustration. The request is clear and direct. The psalmist expects a great and immediate deliverance. The verbs are written in a way that the writer is relying upon God's prior action as proof that God will act now.[21]

- For God to meet us and help—Similar to God acting. We need God to help us in our current situation. Psalm 22:19–20 gives some words to consider when David writes, "But you, Lord, do not be far from me. You are my strength; come quickly to help me. Deliver me from

21. Ross, *Commentary on the Psalms*, 225–26.

the sword, my precious life from the power of the dogs." We want the distance between us and God to go away and we need help!

- For God to vindicate us in our current situation—In sorrow and suffering we can feel that God has allowed unjust people to take advantage of us. When the psalmists felt the same way, they would call upon God for justice. Psalm 83 gives a good example when author writes, "Cover their faces with shame, Lord, so that they will seek your name. May they ever be ashamed and dismayed; may they perish in disgrace. Let them know that you, whose name is the Lord—that you alone are the Most High over all the earth" (Ps 83:16–18). The language here is direct and even a bit vengeful. I am not trying to justify being cruel or over-stepping. However, I am trying to demonstrate that the biblical authors were being honest with God and saying what they really felt and needed.

- For God to forgive our sins—Sometimes we feel that our current situation is no fault of our own. Other times we know that there is sin in our lives that needs to be addressed. By humbling ourselves before God we can make a first step to reconciliation. When David committed adultery with Bathsheba, he prayed Ps 51 as a lament prayer. In verse 1 he writes, "Have mercy on me, O God, according to your unfailing love; according to your great compassion blot out my transgressions. Wash away all my iniquity and cleanse me from my sin. For I know my transgressions, and my sin is always before me. Against you, you only, have I sinned and done what is evil in your sight" (Ps 51:1–4). Only you and God know your sin. A lament prayer is a perfect place to share any shame in your life and step closer into God's light.[22]

- For God to restore us—The central theme of the Bible may well be restoration. In Genesis, God creates mankind. By the end of Gen 3 mankind rejects God, creating a chasm in the relationship. The balance of the Bible is a narrative of restoration between God and humanity ultimately through the death, resurrection, and second coming of Jesus. The psalmists bring this theme into the prayers of lament. David gives us this picture when he writes, "Restore to me the joy of your salvation and grant me a willing spirit, to sustain me" (Ps 51:12).

- For God to listen—A common feeling when we are suffering is to feel that God is not hearing our cries for help. We often feel that if God

22. Kidner, *Psalms 1–71*, 206–7.

could hear us then our circumstance would change—or, at least, we would know that if God were present then we could endure the present suffering. Several psalms convey this idea. David writes, "Listen to my words, Lord, consider my lament" (Ps 5:1). In another psalm we read, "Hear my prayer, Lord, listen to my cry for help; do not be deaf to my weeping" (Ps 39:12).[23]

- For God to teach us—As we reflect upon the word of God during our suffering, we can come to understand that God is teaching us something. Learning from God often means walking in a righteous path. Several psalms include prayerful language to consider. "Guide me in your truth and teach me, for you are God my Savior, and my hope is in you all day long" (Ps 25:5). Another example is when the psalmist writes, "Teach me your way, Lord, that I may rely on your faithfulness; give me an undivided heart, that I may fear your name" (Ps 86:11). Humbling ourselves before God and acknowledging that God knows more than we do is a great step in a lament prayer.

This list is not all inclusive and the Psalms give us many examples of being bold in our communication with God. The keys to praying a lament include an honest, humble, and biblical request that God act in a way that is consistent with his character to bring us through our current pain and suffering.

Some Concluding Thoughts

Sometimes during suffering people realize that they do not have the strength or spiritual ability to go on. They are at the point where there is nothing left except God. This is an opportunity to come along side someone and share the truth about God and Christ.

Sometimes this means sitting with them and saying nothing. Other times, it is an excellent opportunity to pray with them. A prayer of lament might allow you the opportunity to open a dialogue.

The Billy Graham Evangelistic Association recommends some open-ended questions that can start a dialogue, including:[24]

23. Longman and Garland, *Psalms*, 363.
24. Graham, "Sharing Hope in Crisis," 20.

- "How are you holding up?"

- "Where were you when it happened?"

- "What was it like?"

- "I cannot imagine how difficult this is for you."

- "Are you aware of the resources available to you?"

- "Do you have family in the area?"

- "Do you have a church family?"

- "May I pray for you?"

- "Knowing how important faith is at a time like this, could you tell me about your faith?"

The BGEA training goes on to offer seven tips to ministering at a time of crisis and suffering:[25]

- Demonstrate God's compassion.

- Use open questions.

- Help with next steps.

- Are there others involved you could help?

- Are there other issues?

- Avoid distractions.

- Always be prepared to share God's hope.

Vroegop writes that praying alongside a hurting friend is an opportunity to share and strengthen faith. You will likely be able to ask God for help with a deeper level of faith than your hurting friend can muster. The boldness of your request and the confidence in your approach to the throne of grace can be a great help. You can pray with a firm belief that creates stronger faith in others. If you do not know what to pray, consider appealing to God through the words of a lament like Pss 13 or 22. As you echo the boldness of the psalm, it can beget boldness in a hurting friend.[26] In this way, a lament prayer can not only help us. It might also be a tool to share the light of Christ with others during times of suffering.

---

25. Graham, "Sharing Hope in Crisis," 21.

26. Vroegop, *Dark Clouds*, 67.

Bibliography

Anderson, Niel T. *Victory over the Darkness: Realize the Power of Your Identity in Christ.* Revised and Updated Edition. Bloomington, MN: Bethany, 2020.

Billings, Todd. *Rejoicing in Lament: Wrestling with Incurable Cancer and Life in Christ.* Grand Rapids: Brazos, 2015.

Brueggemann, Walter. *Israel's Praise: Doxology against Idolatry and Ideology.* Philadelphia: Fortress, 1971.

Card, Michael. *A Sacred Sorrow: Reaching Out to God in the Lost Language of Lament.* Colorado Springs: NavPress, 2005.

Eklund, Rebekah. "Lord, Teach Us to Grieve: Jesus' Lament and Christian Hope." ThD diss., Duke Divinity School, 2012.

Goldingay, John. *Psalms: Volume 1.* Baker Commentary on the Old Testament. Grand Rapids: Baker Academic, 2006.

Graham, Billy. "Sharing Hope in Crisis." https://rrt.billygraham.org/free-shic-on-demand/.

Kidner, Derek. *Psalms 1–71.* Tyndale Old Testament Commentaries. Downers Grove: InterVarsity, 1973.

Lewis, C. S. *The Problem of Pain.* New York: Collier.

Longman, Tremper, III, and David E. Garland. *Psalms.* The Expositor's Bible Commentary. Rev. ed. Grand Rapids: Zondervan, 1995.

Ross, Allen P. *A Commentary on the Psalms: Volume 1.* Kregel Exegetical Library. Grand Rapids: Kregel, 2011.

VanGemeren, Willem A. *Psalms.* Rev. ed. The Expositor's Bible Commentary. Grand Rapids: Zondervan, 2008.

Vroegop, Mark. *Dark Clouds, Deep Mercy: Discovering the Grace of Lament.* Wheaton: Crossway, 2019.

Westermann, Claus. *Praise and Lament in the Psalms.* Atlanta: John Knox, 1981.

Wolterstorff, Nicolas. *Lament for a Son.* Grand Rapids: Eerdmans, 1987.

Enclosed in the Goodness of God

Julian of Norwich on Prayer

By Grace Hamman, PhD

*Go to your closet in secret prayer and there you
will find peace to your soul.*

—D. L. Moody

Fourteenth-century Europe overflowed with prayers. Everywhere one went in the medieval world one would have heard prayers to Jesus, prayers to the Virgin, prayers to a local saint like Saint John of Beverley or a famous saint like Mary Magdalene or Peter. The clergy and the laity prayed, in short bursts of desperate petitions, in practiced contemplative silences, in the endless, beautiful repetition of the Psalms, at midnight and at noon, in churches, roads, and fields, for the living and the dead. Julian of Norwich speaks from this long-gone setting of abundant devotion, transcending her context to teach us in the twenty-first century how close God truly is in our prayers.

Prayers begin Julian's *A Revelation of Love*. As a young woman, she recalls, Julian had made three requests of God. She prayed to suffer with Jesus, as others did that loved him, "therefore I desired to see the passion with my own eyes, so that I might have more knowledge of the bodily pains of our savior, and the compassion of our lady" (2.10–11).[1] The second: a "willed desire" to have a physical illness, a sickness "hard to the death, that I might in that sickness undergo all the rites of holy church, believing I was about to

---

1. Translations are mine, line numbers from Norwich, *Writings of Julian of Norwich*. When I do not translate, I quote from Watson and Jenkins.

die, and that all who saw me believed it too" (2.18–20). In this ailment, she requests "all manner of pains, physical and spiritual," everything excepting death itself. She clarifies her intentions: "I wanted to be purged by the mercy of God, and ever after live to his worship because of that sickness, so that it would help me when I died" (2.24–26). Finally, she asks to receive three wounds in her life: the wound of true contrition for her sins, the wound of natural compassion, and the wound of desire for God.

Readers who have encountered Julian only through her beloved "hazelnut" vision or her famous teaching "All shall be well" may be disconcerted with the first two prayers that Julian recollects. Today, most of us can hardly imagine praying *for* suffering, particularly bodily suffering. Julian's prayers fit into a particular tradition of the Middle Ages. To ask to see the passion was an accepted practice among both clergy and layfolk wishing to enhance their devotion.[2] By witnessing the sufferings of Jesus, they hoped to increase their love for God and share in those sufferings. The second petition, for an actual physical illness that brings one so near to death's door that they require the last rites and confession, is a little more unusual but still fits into a strong medieval tradition for especially committed lovers of God. Illness was often understood as a purgative aid as one learned to look beyond the pleasures of earth to the promises of heaven for life's true meaning.[3] The body was so often a distracting inconvenience in pursuit of holiness.

Julian's otherworldly prayers are answered, though not in the way that she expects. At the age of thirty, she becomes desperately ill, and believes she is about to die. The priest comes for the last rites and holds the crucifix before her eyes to comfort her as she passes from this life. And to Julian's amazement, the crucifix comes alive. Jesus begins to bleed before her very eyes, and Julian undergoes a night of revelations, seeing and hearing what she calls "showings" from God on the nature of humanity, on Jesus himself, and on prayer.

Julian's writings on prayer can be paradoxical, just like Julian herself. The committed, solitary anchorite uses homely familial metaphors to describe God. Despite earlier praying for special experiences herself, she then pointedly discourages those who would view her contemplative experiences as higher than ordinary petitionary prayer. She prayed for illness to be closer to God and purge her and prepare her for heaven,

2. Medieval manuals taught this practice, like Love, *Mirror of the Blessed Life.*

3. For examples, see Bynum, *Holy Feast and Holy Fast,* esp. ch. 8.

then ultimately uplifts the body as vessel for God's goodness. While not condemning common medieval practices of prayer, Julian broadens and expands the horizons of the prayer that she has been taught. She writes a theology that levels the ingrained hierarchy of medieval prayer and gives grace to the petitioner, however broken, fearful, and incomplete their prayers. She does so by intimately connecting prayer to the incarnation of Jesus and our own bodies. God is closer than our clothes, skin, bones. We, as the people of God past and present, are clad and enclosed in his goodness, and our prayers are rooted in this intimacy. One need not pray for illness in order to be close to God—simultaneously, those prayers are not an impediment to him, either. Julian's God is happily, wonderfully the God present in bodily needs, the God of dirty diapers and washing clothes and broken bones and eating breakfast, as well as the God of revelations, spiritual ecstasy, and sacraments.

Making Many Means: How We Fear to Approach God Directly

Just as people do today, medieval people prayed for a wide variety of desires, in an equally wide variety of ways. Layfolk and clergy alike prayed familiar prayers, simple petitions for healing or in thanksgiving. Also like us, medieval people tried different ways of praying in order to see if some ways worked better than others, in the ultimate hope that their prayers would be heard as they wanted them to be. Sometimes, their prayers were half plea, half spell, as they repeated prayers a magical number of times, made signs with their hands, walked in a pattern, or entreated particular saints with pledges of reward or good behavior. Many medieval people promised God a pilgrimage or gifts to a shrine or church, if they were healed of an ailment or if a special event came to pass.[4]

Julian writes with compassion, not judgment, about these practices. With characteristic clear-sightedness, she recognizes that much of the "custom" of medieval prayer actually consists of means that reveal a mistrust or hesitance to approach God directly:

> The custom of our prayer was brought to my mind: how that for unknowing of love, we make many means. Then I saw truthfully that it is more worship and delight to God, that we faithfully pray to himself, cleaving to his goodness by his grace, with true

4. Resources on medieval English prayer: Duffy, *Stripping of the Altars*; Scott-Stokes, *Women's Books of Hours*.

> understanding and steadfast belief, than if we made all the means
> our hearts could imagine. (6.2–7)

When Julian says "means," she means the contrivances we as petition-ers adopt in order to feel close in prayer or increase the likelihood that our prayers have been heard. Julian lists the ways that people hesitatingly approach God: through invoking his holy flesh and precious blood, through his blessed mother and her love, through the holy cross on which he died, and with all the help of all the saints and their endless friendship. We invoke means in prayer because of our "unknowing of love." Unaware of or unable to accept the truth of God's love, more focused on his wrath and their own insignificance or sinfulness, people waver to speak to Jesus directly and simply present their requests to God.

It's easy to critically judge these "customs of prayer," especially today as a postmodern Protestant. These "means" are not applicable only to me-dieval folk or to Roman Catholics or Christians within "high" theological traditions. Protestants too approach God through means, like strictly regi-mented quiet times (read the Bible, pray, journal) or a specialized vocabu-lary. Even voices and mannerisms can become crutches on which to lean as we pray. Those of us who are more judgmental (including myself) have cringed at pastors with special, extra solemn praying voices.

Though she notes they stem from "unknowing of love," Julian does not view these means with contempt. Unlike the later Protestant reformers, Julian's concerns about means are not that they are heretical or damaging, but that they can cloud the essential truth of God's presence in his people's prayers. We are not praying to a distant God enthroned in heaven, sur-rounded by supplicating saints and attended by his mother and disciples. He is present, closer than our own bodies. In a surprising twist, she pro-claims that some of these means have also been ordained by God through his goodness to help us. At first glance, this statement seems to contradict her earlier words. But the gracious God looks mercifully upon human weak-ness. The principle means that helps us perceive our closeness to God and understand his work on earth, she writes, is the incarnation. The human face of Jesus helps us pray. How can we understand this seeming about-face? Through her invocation of the incarnation, we realize that means and ways are crutches in a double sense: we use them to get to God, or to cajole him, when we are not confident, he will receive us; but we also use them to hobble in all our limitations into the love of the Godhead. Julian teaches that God is big enough. Our contrivances of prayer are no impediment to him, and he views them in his everlasting mercy and compassion. He even offers some himself, with compassion for our human weakness and feelings of insecurity. Ways into prayer can be gifts used in appreciation or obstacles used with fear. The incarnation is not a new love, but a means to understand a preexisting Love, the Love that moves the sun and stars and yet also dwells with us here on earth.

"The Lowest Part of Our Need": No Prayer Is Too Abject For God's Goodness

This unfailing closeness and goodness of God becomes Julian's main point on prayer: "For the goodness of God is the highest prayer, and it comes down to us, to the lowest part of our need." What does she mean when she writes "the goodness of God is the highest prayer"? Such a question brings up the problem of form and content. How do we pray? What counts as good prayer? These questions are also in Julian's mind. In this line, Julian refers to the grace of contemplation, the particular type of prayer that concerns meditating extensively upon the goodness and character of God. Contemplation was the work of anchorites, visionaries, mystics, and monks. Contemplatives withdrew from the busy world in order to practice their craft of prayer. Julian herself, as we can remember from her beginning prayers, wished to become one of these gifted contemplatives, endowed with "mind of the passion" and special suffering given by God.

There was a clear hierarchy of prayer and of pray-ers for medieval thinkers. For some men and women, prayer was their profession. Chantries were groups of male clergy hired to pray in perpetuity for the dead in purgatory. Monks and nuns would wake wearily in the middle of the night to sing and pray. Anchorites, like Julian herself became after her near-death experience, were literally walled into their parish church, a process overseen by a bishop performing the rites of the dead. That was the exact idea: anchorites, mostly women, had died to the world and now only lived for the spiritual life of Christ. They spent their days immersed in the liturgy and sacraments, which they could see and participate in through a window in their cell. The laity imitated these monastic practices, especially women. Some laywomen famously practiced contemplative prayer and received visions from God, like Catherine of Siena, Bridget of Sweden, or Margery Kempe.

It was widely accepted that contemplative prayer was superior to the prayer of beseeching and asking, a Mary far surpassing the Martha worried about the cares of the world. According to this model, the monks, hermits, and anchorites who spent their life contemplating God were spiritually superior to the plowmen, mothers, fishmongers, blacksmiths, alewives, and ditch-diggers who had no time in their busy earthly lives to contemplate, who sent up simple prayers for children to be healed or ships to come safe to harbor. Most people considered the prayers of the contemplatives who saw visions of Jesus or Mary and cast aside the needs of their body to pursue God's wisdom, as far superior to those who lived the active life in the world with their mundane or even sacrilegious petitionary prayers. Drawing on eminent medieval theologians like Bernard of Clairvaux, Julian's contemporary writers on prayer urged their readers to leave the material world behind as they ascended closer to God through contemplative prayer.[5] Julian writes into a landscape of expert pray-ers, who present prayer and the Christian life in hierarchical systems of degrees, ladders, or steps. Works like the English *The Scale of Perfection* by Walter Hilton or the influential Latin *The Four Degrees of Violent Love* by Richard of Saint Victor both uphold hierarchical models of the life of prayer and love of God even in their very titles.

Though Julian upholds the value of contemplative prayer ("the goodness of God is the highest prayer"), she complicates the tradition as she turns to a rather shocking example of how, exactly, that prayer works. She now turns to explicating the second half of that sentence: the goodness of God, the highest prayer, comes to us *in the lowest part of our need*. Instead of transcending the body, prayer works in our very sinews and muscles and skin, in our guts:

A man walks upright, and the food he eats is contained and held in his body as in a drawstring bag. And when it is necessary, the bag is cleanly and efficiently opened and emptied. God showed that *he* does this, when it was said: "He comes down to us, to the lowest part of our need." For he has no contempt for what he has made, nor has he disdain to serve us at the most natural and simplest function of our body, all for the love of the soul that he has made in his own likeness. For as the body is clad in the cloth, and the flesh in the skin, and the bones in the flesh, and the heart in the trunk, so are we, soul and body, clad and enclosed in the goodness of God (6.25–37).

5. Helpful resources on medieval contemplative prayer and Julian include: Nuth, *God's Lovers*; Turner, *Julian of Norwich, Theologian*, esp. ch. 5.

The goodness of God, the highest prayer, reveals itself in the most vulgar of human needs: digestion and defecation. She reorients our understanding of human waste; she describes it providentially, as God's goodness in designing our bodies to elegantly and neatly dispel waste after consumption. Even bowel movements are miraculous revelations of God's love and mercy.

Medieval Christians (or postmodern!) did not typically use defecation as an example of God's goodness. Nor did they have a particularly high opinion of feces. In fact, penitential works—texts meant to stimulate reflection on one's sinfulness, so that one could confess and repent with honesty and contrition—often use fecal language to describe human works and bodies. For example, the contemporaneous penitential work *Jacob's Well* tells readers that they are each a "sack full of dung," and reminds them to cultivate shame.[6] The tradition that considers the body a *vas stercorum*, a bag of excrement (which could be translated even more vulgarly!), is long and storied.[7] In contrast, Julian unashamedly embraces the grossest of bodily functions as a reminder of God's tender and clever care, not humanity's intrinsically foul nature.

It was a provocative choice to set the elevated discourse of contemplation alongside the degrading functions of bodies. Many of Julian's contemporary thinkers on prayer disapproved of any bodily language in relation to contemplation, and some of any illustrating examples of God's goodness at all. The anonymous author of *The Cloud of Unknowing* argues that though it can be good "sometimes" to think on the concrete goodness of God in the life of Christ or the passion, such thoughts must be "cast down and covered with a cloud of forgetting" in order for the would-be contemplative to truly remember how unknowable God is and to pierce ever closer to that mystery.[8]

When Julian marries the language of contemplation to our bodily functions, she smashes value-oriented distinction between prayer as contemplation, the vocation of the educated or specially blessed, and prayer as mere needy petition, the work of the uneducated layfolk mired in the material world. She insists both are valuable and intrinsic to the Christian life. The separation between these modes of prayer is artificial: the

---

6. Brandeis, *Jacob's Well*, 236.

7. Jones, "'To Embrace a Sack of Excrement,'" 662–98.

8. Gallacher, *Cloud of Unknowing*, 6.461; 7.490.

goodness of God is the highest prayer, *and* it comes down to us, to the lowest part of our need.

As we read, we may be tempted to dismiss Julian's reflections because in American Protestant Christian traditions, we no longer consciously subscribe to hierarchies of prayer or of manners of living. Postmodern readers don't generally consider contemplative prayer and those who practice it as superior to those who live in the world and practice petitionary prayer. But we still have hierarchies: American Christianity tends to elevate families over single folks, or people who work hard in the "real world" as more valuable than those who cloister themselves officially or unofficially in order to pray full-time. We still succumb to hierarchies that prize some life and prayer experiences more than others. And Julian's next demolition of prayer values may feel more familiar. Christians may believe, consciously or unconsciously, that those who encounter God more concretely are closer to him or more beloved by him.

"I Had Him and I Wanted Him": God Is Close, Regardless of Our Feelings

After a terrifying sequence in *Revelation* where Julian witnesses Jesus's bodily suffering, she asks God for more light in order to see better and understand. God does not give her more light. Instead, he responds that he will be her light. She concludes, "So I saw him and sought him, and I had him and lacked him; and this is and should be our common working in this life, as I see it" (10.14). By common, she could mean daily and/or frequent, or universal, and she involves a paradox. We have God, though we often don't know it; even when we see him, it feels like he may not be there. Our searching, yearning, unfulfilled desire for him is generative, though not in the ways we may expect.

In the old medieval system, some writers believed that their increasing holiness would be revealed in feelings of closeness to God. Richard Rolle, a hermit and very popular English writer on prayer, wrote of warmth, suffusive joy, even beautiful melodies that accompanied his experiences of God's love in his prayers.[9] Julian herself wished desperately to participate in another and less obviously enjoyable medieval experience of God's closeness in prayer: to share in Christ's own suffering by witnessing the passion. Some, like Saint Francis of Assisi, even received stigmata—what medieval

9. Rolle, *Richard Rolle.*

people understood as the highest gift of unity and identification with Jesus, the wounds of the cross on their hands and feet. These experiences, though not universal, were all part of the contemplative tradition of medieval prayer. To use Julian's own language, *beholding* was the climax of contemplative prayer, the moment where God gives a special grace to his lovers of witnessing some aspect of himself, either historically as in passion visions, or through feelings of joy, peace, or pleasurable sensory experiences. Unity or extreme closeness with God flowers in a moment beyond time. In other words, such an experience is what we today primarily associate with the idea of mysticism. This is what Julian, as a young woman, desired so deeply that she prayed to suffer in order to experience it.

What I love about Julian is that she *does* receive a vision of the passion, she does have a particular experience with God that few others can lay claim to, as she requested—but she begins to understand that anything she experiences can and should be applied to all whom God loves. Her showings are not a mark of special favor, and in fact, if they are understood as such, they are worthless (Julian would have a lot to say about the #blessed hashtag and the prosperity gospel today). Julian ends up stating bluntly: "seeking is as good as beholding, for the time that [God] allows the soul to be in labor" (10.62–63). Quite simply, this is because seeking and beholding depend on our limited human perceptions. God is there, regardless of whether the person feels it or not.

Though God does will us to perceive him, and we will in this life or the next, beholding is not superior to seeking. Seeking, or petitionary prayer, is the human condition built into our very souls as individual people. In fact, Julian writes, the soul cannot do more than to "seek, suffer, and trust" (10.55). Julian would've heartily agreed with the twentieth-century theologian and author on prayer, Harry Emerson Fosdick, who in 1915 wrote,

Samuel Johnson once was asked what the strongest argument for prayer was, and he replied, "Sir, there is no argument for prayer." One need only read Johnson's own petitions, such as the one below, to see that he did not mean by this to declare prayer irrational; he meant to stress the fact that praying is first of all a native tendency. It is a practice like breathing or eating in this respect, that men engage in it because they are human, and *afterward* argue about it as best they can.[10]

Breathing, praying, seeking. The soul reaches out as a natural function of our creation. The Creator God values seeking as much as unitive beholding;

10. Fosdick, *Meaning of Prayer*, 1.

this equal valuation graciously levels distinctions between people. My five-year old daughter, a junior metaphysician who asks questions like if Jesus could breathe underwater, is just as holy and blessed as, say, the profound seeker *and* beholder Saint Augustine of Hippo. Of course, it doesn't necessarily mean that she possesses as much wisdom or insight as Augustine, but her prayers are wrought of the same gold as the great Bishop's.

Julian resists theologies of prayer that prize *outcomes* of prayer—visions, even just spiritual feelings of fulfillment or joy, or the ability to suffer with Christ on the cross—over the basic sense of seeking conversation between God and a person. Holiness is not dependent on these moments of spiritual fulfillment. As humans, it's hard for us to see that. We want feelings of transcendence as proof that we are close to God. While most postmodern folk do not long for stigmata today, we want other signs and the distinction of being set apart through our prayerful encounters with the divine. It's easy to see the merit in these experiences and value them, and the people who experience them, above the common herd. Sometimes we receive these gifts, sometimes we do not. But they are not indicative of God's closeness, nor of the generative capacities of our conversations with God. To seek God is our function as humans.

Just as God is in our lowest needs as well as our highest moments of contemplation, God is just as much in the seeking as in the beholding. And in her longest section on prayer, Julian writes that we must learn to trust both our own littleness and God's encompassing presence in both bowels and souls.

"Rightful Prayer" and Complete Trust: Praying as Participation in Creation

Thus far, against much of her culture, Julian insists that God has no disdain of his creation in their feeble attempts to reach out to him. The simplest petitionary prayer is just as valuable as transcendental contemplative moments on the love of God. The needs of the body and the needs of the soul are both providentially cared for by God. The prayers of the child or atheist who prays in a whim or panic of the moment are just as precious to him as the ecstasy and love of the most profound mystical theologian who has witnessed the passion itself. Chapters 41–42 of *A Revelation of Love* could be called Julian's treatise on prayer. This section especially considers the attitude that we should adopt in prayer, the attitude that best reflects how much

God truly loves us and listens to us. Julian considers what she calls the two conditions of prayer: rightful prayer and secure trust.

She tackles the point directly: our trust is not complete. We're not certain that God hears us because of our unworthiness, and because we feel nothing. We can be as desert-dry after our prayers as we were before them. She knows because she has felt that way herself (41.3–5). In response, the Lord answers her: "I am the ground of your beseeching. First it is my will that you have it, and then I make you to will it, and then I make you to ask it—and you ask it! How should it be then that you not receive what you ask for?" (41.8–10). God's words to Julian do not mean if I pray for a beach house in San Diego that God has put that desire into my heart and I will receive it. Nor do they mean that we are automatons, controlled by God in our every whim.

First, Julian extrapolates that our prayer is not the cause of God's goodness to us. We do not change his mind and thereby change history through our prayers. God's goodness is the cause of his goodness (41.19–20). Relatedly, she articulates a theology close to Thomas Aquinas's doctrine that we are created to desire the good and we naturally tend towards the beauty and goodness revealed in creation that offers a hint of God's vast, surpassing love. We are made to desire beauty, truth, and goodness. In our prayers, we plead for those in varying forms as we recognize them in our human limitations. She writes, "Beseeching is a true, gracious, lasting will of the soul, united and fastened into the will of our Lord by the sweet, secret working of the Holy Spirit" (41.24–25). Though its outer form may be skewed, in its deepest form our will is aligned with God's will, which becomes evident the more that we pray in Jesus's loving name. This is what Julian calls "rightful prayer." In this sense, Julian argues that all prayer, no matter how stupid, trivial, or wrong in its content, is rightful prayer. One's actions or thoughts around these prayers may not be rightful. But when a person honestly approaches God with trust and beseeches him, even if the content of one's prayer relates to the lowest need, Julian believes one's desire for the love and goodness embedded in God comes to the forefront. This prayer God will always answer with joy because he has made that desire within his people, in his image.

For Julian, the image of the child best reveals how Jesus sees his people. Children are not afraid to ask, even if it's something trivial. This can be frustrating for parents, as they witness their child asking with complete hope and confidence for a candy bar, then having an utter meltdown in

Safeway as her request is denied. If a child requests of her parent something that she yearns for out of her desire for beauty and goodness and truth, won't a parent do anything in their power to give that goodness to their child, in the form that is best for them from the adult's more encompassing perspective? Then, it is the task of the parent to teach their child how to desire the good and right thing with more accuracy and depth. When the child requests the candy bar, she is following her natural desire for delicious goodness, *and* showing her confidence that her parent wants to give her good things. When the parent says no in that moment, she promises the child that there are better things than this candy bar: health and pain-free visits to the dentist, and perhaps an even better treat after dinner in moderation and enjoyment. But the child's request itself was, essentially, a good one for fulfillment and joy, gifts that the good parent also wills for the child and tries to answer in fullness.

Why then ask at all? Wouldn't it be better if the Lord perceived these needs and taught us before we prayed? It's not a question of capability; he certainly could do that. But as any good teacher or parent knows, the richest and most rewarding transformations occur when students participate and even take the lead in their own learning processes. *Praying is an act of co-creation in Julian's theology.* From the smallest child's prayer (my son Simon inexplicably thanks God "for the bushes" at dinner every day), to the Magnificat itself, our prayers allow us to participate in the pleasure and privilege of spiritual formation and the creation of good in the world. We become more like Jesus through our own prayers and expressed desire. God graciously shares this joy with us. In the lighthearted example of the candy bar, the child learns how to take care of her body as she asks for candy bars in the checkout aisle. She is a beloved participant in her creation as a growing human.

And as with children who are afraid of their parents, doubt and fear can impede people from asking in this open way for love and the fulfillment of need. We fear we won't receive what we want. We fear we won't be heard, so we make means. People seek to find the *best* method of prayer, one that makes them feel closest to God or holiest from a given perspective. And this is largely because many Christians, Julian understands, have a mental image of God that does not focus the enormity and capability of God's love. Joan Nuth writes,

Prayer always contains an element of self-donation, an acknowledgment of the need for a 'higher power' to come to one's aid. But such an act of self-donation or expression of need can only be done from an attitude of trust. Thus one's image of God is absolutely crucial. If one imagines God as a stern judge, distant and far away, difficult to please, such an attitude of trust is practically impossible. But if one imagines God as someone who loves unconditionally, no matter how much one sins, then it is possible to approach God in trust, expecting to be accepted and helped.[11]

Julian lays such emphasis on trust in her treatise on prayer because it is the lack of trust that keeps one from approaching God with honesty and all needs. Throughout the rest of *Revelation*, she will explore different images of God in order to help her readers learn to trust in God's unwavering love and compassion for his creation. Her visions of God as an exceptionally courteous and shockingly humble Lord or an attentive, loving Mother create alternative images for a people used to envisioning him as furious with them in their vast selfishness, or at best begrudgingly intervening *again* in their catastrophic, often idiotic failures. But Julian saw everything through the lens of the passion and the God who willingly and lovingly suffered for every person. She knows it is this God who is present with us in our very bodies and neediest prayers.

"He Ever Keeps Us in His Blessed Love": A Last Word on Christ's Nearness in Suffering

Julian's theology of prayer beautifully gives room to those in pain, those who feel far from God, and those who have strived mightily for holiness but are weary and uncertain. She has dwelt in these moments herself, and is determined to share that though these feelings are dark and horrible, they are no impediment to Jesus. What happens when you cannot pray? There have been periods in my life where it has been near impossible for me to pray. While pregnant with my first child, I suffered an intense bout of pre-natal depression that destroyed my ability to focus. As a graduate student, this loss felt particularly devastating, as if an essential part of myself had disappeared overnight. I could not listen to teaching in class or sermons at church. I could not write. I could not pray. All I could do was show up, with my growing belly, open my hands to take communion, and place Christ's body in my mouth with a certain blankness. All my motivation, all my innate cleverness, all my capacity for feeling goodness had been drained from my mind and body. The only thing I really felt was a bitter guilt for my

11. Nuth, *God's Lovers*, 111.

sadness when I had such good things in my life: I was about to have a baby I desired with a husband I loved in our very first house. I had friends who wanted a baby so much who had not received one. There were people starving and dying and homeless in the world. I hated myself.

I would like to tell you that Julian's words were part of my journey towards mental health, but I would be lying. I certainly was not able to focus enough to read her complex, medieval writing. There was no fix for me other than giving birth. But Julian's theology of prayer speaks to my experience. *The goodness of God is the highest prayer, and it comes to us in the lowest part of our needs.* God's presence with me goes deeper than my mind, or my mental capacities, or my ability to receive truth. Julian tells me those all end up being means, anyway. They can be great gifts or further obstacles, maybe even both at the same time. God is in my gut, in my very creation from the beginning of time, and even if my prayers go no higher than my bodily suffering, he hears them with love. Like Julian, I want to trust the crucified God. His love for his people is not contingent on their response to him, on their prayers, on their limited minds or flawed bodies. The good incarnate God is intimately acquainted with the limitations and suffering inextricable from embodiment.

> And also our good lord showed that it is full great pleasure to him that a simple soul come to him nakedly, plainly, and homely. For this is the natural yearning of the soul by the touching of the Holy Ghost, which I understand by this showing: "God, of thy goodness, give me thyself. For thou art enough to me, and I may ask nothing that is less that may be full worship to thee. And if I ask anything that is less, ever me wanteth. But only in thee I have all." And these words, "God of thy goodness," are full lovesome to the soul, and full near touch the will of our Lord. For his goodness comprehendeth all his creatures and all his blessed works and overpasseth without end. For he is the endlesshead, and he hath made us only to himself and restored us by his precious passion, and ever keepeth us in his blessed love. And all this is of his goodness. (5.28–38)

Bibliography

Brandeis, Arthur, ed. *Jacob's Well: An English Treatise on the Cleansing of Man's Conscience.* London: Paul, Trench, Trubner, 1900.

Bynum, Caroline Walker. *Holy Feast and Holy Fast: The Religious Significance of Food to Medieval Women.* Berkeley, CA: University of California Press, 1988.

Duffy, Eamon. *The Stripping of the Altars: Traditional Religion in England, C. 1400–C.1580.* New Haven, CT: Yale University Press, 2005.

Fosdick, Harry Emerson. *The Meaning of Prayer.* New York: Association Press, 1949.

Gallacher, Patrick J., ed. *The Cloud of Unknowing.* Kalamazoo, MI: Medieval Institute Publications, Western Michigan University Press, 2005.

Jones, Christopher A. "'To Embrace a Sack of Excrement': Odo of Cluny and the History of an Image." *Speculum* 96 (2021) 662–98.

Julian of Norwich. *The Writings of Julian of Norwich: A Vision Showed to a Devout Woman and A Revelation of Love.* Edited by Nicholas Watson and Jacqueline Jenkins. University Park, PA: Pennsylvania State University Press, 2006.

Love, Nicholas. *The Mirror of the Blessed Life of Jesus Christ: A Reading Text.* Edited by Michael G. Sargent. Exeter, UK: University of Exeter Press, 2004.

Nuth, Joan. *God's Lovers in an Age of Anxiety: The Medieval English Mystics.* London: Darton, Longman & Todd, 2001.

Rolle, Richard. *Richard Rolle: The English Writings.* Translated by Rosamund S. Allen. New York: Paulist, 1988.

Scott-Stokes, Charity. *Women's Books of Hours in Medieval England: Selected Texts Translated from Latin, Anglo-Norman French, and Middle English with Introduction and Interpretive Essay.* Woodbridge, UK: Brewer, 2012.

Turner, Denys. *Julian of Norwich, Theologian.* New Haven, CT: Yale University Press, 2011.

At Home among the Trees

Prayer from the Heart of the Earth

By ASHISH VARMA, PhD

*A great many people are afraid of the will of God, and yet I
believe that one of the sweetest lessons that we can learn in the
school of Christ is the surrender of our wills to God, letting Him
plan for us and rule our lives.*

—D. L. MOODY

"Praise the Lord from the earth,
you great sea creatures and all ocean depths, . . .
your mountains and all hills,
    fruit trees and all cedars." —Ps 148:7, 9

"When you hide your face,
    they are terrified;
when you take away their breath,
    they die and return to the dust.
When you give your Breath,
    they are created,
    and you renew the face of the ground." —Ps 104:29–30

"Praise be You, my Lord, with all your creatures. . . .
"Praise be You, my Lord, through our Sister Mother Earth,
who sustains and governs us,
and who produces varied fruits with colored flowers and herbs."

—Saint Francis of Assisi

In his famous "The Canticle of Brother Sun," medieval friar Saint Francis of Assisi offers one of the most important markers for his enduring legacy. Known through Christian tradition for his habit of preaching to the animals, beckoning them to turn to their Creator, Francis here offers his poetic rendition of the call for all of creation to praise God. Each short section highlights an element of creation—such as the wind—and its role in serving the cosmos to the praise of God. It is hardly surprising to realize that Francis comes from an era of the church's history that more quickly understood every created thing to belong to a delicately and wisely designed creation, at their best serving each other in the grand movement of creation toward God. In fact, the procession of God into creation—the Son to redeem and the Spirit to enliven—was a divine work to reset all of creation into unity and balance so that it could return to its true (supernatural) movement toward God. In that sense, Francis's beckoning of creation to praise God fits more easily into contemporary Christian readings of biblical passages such as Psalm 148. Creation *testifies* to God, which we today generally read metaphorical. Creation "speaks" in the sense that it offers evidence for its Creator and makes its fullest sense in light of the existence of the all-mighty and all-benevolent God, even if creation cannot really "speak" the way humanity does. For us, the testimony of creation usually serves apologetics, the defense of Christian faith through defense of our confession of the existence of the holy Trinity.

On further examination, though, Francis seems to be saying more. He seems to be more directly and intentionally calling upon the creatures of the earth to praise God. He is quite comfortable believing that each member of creation has a voice that can call out to God. At first blush, we modern readers are inclined to laugh at his eccentricity—or worse, scoff at his childishness. Perhaps if we are in a more generous place, we will embrace Francis's whimsy in the above metaphorical form, directing we image bearers of God—we *homo divinus*—to praise God. Just as the earth and the cosmos, indeed all that God has made, "declare the glory of God" by the sheer intricacy of their design and the complexity of their interdependence, all the more ought we to turn to God, the Maker of all, and proclaim his goodness and grandeur.

In fact, we should look to creation and gain our cues from it. We ought to trust God in the way that the birds do for their food and the flowers do for their clothing (Matt 6:26–30). We ought to look to the ant and follow the lead of its steady dedication to the important tasks it serves for its colony

(Prov 6:6–8). We ought to mind the trees and be grateful for the fruit it provides for us and other creatures of the earth (Deut 20:19). But before all of these points of practicality, we ought to attend to creation as the community of what Norman Wirzba calls our "enmeshing." In what follows, I will argue that we are creatures who irreducibly belong to the earth, which should deliberately be the setting from which we call out to God. Saint Francis's "Canticle" presents more than material for apologetics or a metaphorical call to pray in the presence of the wonder of creation. Rather, he rightly recognizes the prayer of creation itself, and the calls for the creatures who bear God's image to pray precisely from within the earth by the Holy Breath that gives live to all the earth. In fact, our prayer takes on new contours of compassion and sympathy—the hallmarks of biblical love—precisely when we are able to turn to God from within our places in creation. I will pay special attention to the trees, which hold a special place in the stories of creation and new creation, and to the breath of God that the Christian Scriptures deliberately couple with the breath of the earth that passes between God's animate creatures and the trees. Earth and breath belong together, and both are the preconditions of our prayer.

Creatures of the Earth

Treebeard: Metaphor or Voice of the Forest?

In his contemporary classic, *The Lord of the Rings*, philologist and fantasy author J. R. R. Tolkien constructs a world of fantastic creatures of many varieties. He describes some of these creatures to be nearly as old as the world itself, though unknown to most of the current inhabitants. These ancient creatures generally bear the marks of wisdom and sorrow, for they have experienced the tumultuous breaking of the world many times over and sometimes bear the scars in their bodies. Not all ancient creatures project wisdom in Tolkien's world, but those that do fit well the remark of the Teacher in Ecclesiastes: "Then I applied myself to the understanding of wisdom, and also of madness and folly, but I learned that this, too, is a chasing after the wind. For with much wisdom comes much sorrow; the more knowledge, the more grief (1:17–18).

Among the oldest of these creatures in Tolkien's mythic world is a race of tree herders known as "Ents," who themselves resemble the trees. Perhaps the wisest is Treebeard, and predictably, he also bears the marks of sorrow. He has seen the earth change, from the loss of loved ones to the loss of a sense of harmony among God's creatures. Few cared about the trees anymore, and as a result, the forests had gained a reputation of dark mystery. Some of this reputation is certainly deserved in Tolkien's fictive world, for evil creatures take residence in many dark parts of several forests. However, Tolkien's message is clear: the evil residency was not inevitable; such creatures found homes in the forests because the various peoples of Middle Earth had grown alienated from the trees. Most of these peoples had long abandoned attempts to understand the trees, and the result was a growing sense of fear over their now strange groans. Long gone were the ancient friendships with Ents and trees. Fear wrought suspicion and an inability to understand the speech of the forest and even the trees themselves. For Tolkien, this loss was a tragedy that cut to the core of the being of the peoples of Middle Earth. Loss of understanding was loss of connection to the depths of their own humanity. *The disconnection made evil inevitable* in every corner and crevice of the human heart and creation.

As with Francis's "Canticle," modern readers are inclined to dismiss such stories as the "escapist" literature of mere fantasy. Such descriptions of trees are figments of the imagination, where "imagination" is completely disconnected from the "real." It is precisely this charge that Tolkien confronts in his famous essay "On Fairy-Stories," where he argues for the importance of imagination and the fantastical as means of awakening people to the depths of wonder at the heart of God's creation. That things seem strange in fairy stories is a good thing—indeed, it "is a virtue not a vice."[1] After all, the fantastical can provide a way to "survey the depths of space and time" and to awake the possibility of "communion with other living things."[2] For Tolkien, among the most treasured arenas of reawakened communion was with the creatures of the earth itself. He writes that closest to the heart of the "true purposes of Faërie" was its ability to narrate a "magical understanding by men of the proper languages of birds and beasts and trees."[3] His choice of words here is significant. Tolkien does not ascribe the magical power to the naming of speech among animals and among trees. He takes for granted that they can talk. The fantastical element of his stories is that the peoples of Middle Earth sometimes understand the speech. And sure enough, the most virtuous characters in his tale, more

1. Tolkien, "On Fairy-Stories," 139.
2. Tolkien, "On Fairy-Stories," 116.
3. Tolkien, "On Fairy-Stories," 117.

often than not, are numbered among those who patiently lend their ears to animals and trees and who lovingly care for them. Meanwhile, the most ruthless in Middle Earth regularly mangle animals for ill purposes. Similarly, these same peoples fell trees in mass, seeing them as nuisances that take up valuable real estate. At best, the wicked tend to see trees as raw materials awaiting some greater perfection within their designs. But for them, there is no personal connection to the trees.

Treebeard has seen the entire spectrum of relations between people and trees. He befriends Gandalf, the angelic "wizard" sent to stir up the hearts of people against evil. Initially, he does the same with Saruman, another angelic being on a similar divine mission. However, unlike Gandalf, Saruman loses his way. One of his first acts in his coming out as a force of domination rather than a servant of love is to fell trees in mass. His brutality toward and objectification of trees prefigured his brutality to the peoples of Middle Earth, for the two brutalities belong together for Tolkien. Treebeard takes notice and comments that Saruman should know better. Treebeard notes that Saruman used to walk through the forests, communing with the Ents and trees. Now his silence toward the forest is deafening. Saruman had lost ears to hear, so to speak, and with his ears went understanding of the voices and needs of the trees and of the peoples around him.

But what are we to make of Tolkien's story? Should we follow him and Anselm and listen for the voices of the trees, or should we take his musings metaphorically, calling us from a distance to care about God's creation without ascribing agency of testimony to them? Do trees really talk? German arborist Peter Wohlleben may aid us. In his widely popular work *The Hidden Life of Trees*, he conveys his lifetime of experience as a professional caretaker of trees in German forests in addition to his study of trees in general. Among the many wonders that he describes, perhaps most impressive is the versatility through which trees communicate with each other and even with humans. Perhaps the most basic form of speech takes place through the roots, wherein trees distinguish among their kinds. On a general level, forest trees of the same species stick together by negotiating their use of space. Their intertangled roots reach toward each other, recognize friend, and communicate boundaries for branch growth at the canopy of the tree high above the forest floor. They are far less accommodating toward other tree species—"non-friends"—choosing to concentrate growth in their direction. The careful cooperative work among friend trees results in efficient occupation of space to maximize access to sunlight, which in turn creates a tight communion below and above ground to protect the friends from otherwise dangerous winds in storms.[4]

Wohlleben even notes the contrast between the natural growth forests, where the trees bond through their roots, and commercial forest plantations, where trees are more carefully controlled and moved in order to create efficient forest landscapes to maximize lumber commodity. In these latter settings, the "roots are irreparably damaged when they are planted," thereby preventing the sort of communication seen in the natural forest. As a result, trees in the commercial forests "behave like loners and suffer from their isolation." They more easily fall in storms and act only in their own self-interest in the construction of their canopies. In the absence of their communication, the trees are worse off.[5]

Matters get even more interesting within a tree "family." Wohlleben describes a maternal process in which the older mother tree deliberately protects and communicates with her daughter tree. The canopy that the mother tree creates in collaboration with her friends prevents almost all sunlight from reaching the forest floor. Normally the inability to conduct photosynthesis on a massive scale would signal the impending death of a tree. However, mother trees seemingly deliberately deprive light from their children at their base. The result is a slow growth for the young tree, which means few air pockets in the trunk. The compacted cells in the trunk enable a sturdy base as the tree grows, both enabling it to endure strong windstorms and removing space where fungus might infiltrate and decimate the tree from the inside. But how do the young trees survive with so little sunlight to convert into sugar? The mother trees in natural forests provide nutrients to the daughter trees through intertwined root systems. The young tree can grow slowly and deliberately until the mother tree finally communicates the time of rapid growth to her offspring by opening gaps in her canopy.[6] Again, the communicative process is awe-inspiring.

But so far, the "communication" has been entirely through electrical impulses in the roots.[7] To speak of "voices" here still seems metaphorical. Wohlleben goes on to describe visual and olfactory means of communication through the use of colorful flowers and pleasant aromas to lure bees and

4. Wohlleben, *Hidden Life of Trees*, 4–5.

5. Wohlleben, *Hidden Life of Trees*, 5.

6. Wohlleben, *Hidden Life of Trees*, 32–35.

7. Wohlleben, *Hidden Life of Trees*, 12.

pungent odors to repel harmful insects.[8] Additionally, though Wohlleben describes communicative noises, one type takes the form of crackling in the roots that might otherwise sound random, similar to the crackling of air escaping from a bowl of cereal and milk. However, Wohlleben relays the surprised observations of researchers, who noticed that the crackling of the roots at a consistent frequency of 220 hertz coincided with the reorientation of roots in other trees and plants both nearby and in neighboring laboratory areas. The researchers replicated the noise at the same frequency, and each time, the roots of trees and other plants responded by "orienting their tips in that direction." That is, the roots were listening for instructions.[9]

Other researchers have noted similar phenomena. In one setting, when deprived of water, researchers registered ultrasonic "screams" coming from the trees, as though they were crying out in thirst. Wohlleben suggests that the "trees might be screaming out a dire warning to their colleagues that water levels are running low."[10] For our purposes, in light of such biblical passages as Ps 148 and Saint Francis's suggestion, might the trees also be crying out to their maker, much as people in dire hunger and thirst pray for deliverance? In the Gospel of Luke, Jesus declares that even if humanity neglects to testify concerning him, the "stones will cry out" (19:40). If stone can cry out in testimony of their Maker, cannot the trees cry out to him for deliverance?

Finally, it would seem that on some level, we have the capacity to hear the chatter of the trees. Wohlleben recounts other studies that compared the effect of the trees on people strolling through natural and commercial forests. Healthy natural forests had the effect of increased health in people: lowered blood pressure, increased lung capacity, and the "elasticity of their arteries improved." Wohlleben suggests that the "swirling cocktail of tree talk is the reason we enjoy being out in the forest so much." The people themselves felt the positive effects. Meanwhile, commercial forests, full of angst and "alarm calls" from the loner trees, had the opposite effect on people.[11] Again for our purposes, might we suggest that our subconscious ability to hear the voices of the forest, whether in peace or in angst, enables us on one hand to join into the harmony of voices, most notably those singing

---

8. Wohlleben, *Hidden Life of Trees*, 11–12; Robin Wall Kimmerer describes a similar phenomenon of communication among pecan trees in *Braiding Sweetgrass*, 11–21.

9. Wohlleben, *Hidden Life of Trees*, 13.

10. Wohlleben, *Hidden Life of Trees*, 48.

11. Wohlleben, *Hidden Life of Trees*, 223.

praises to their Creator, and on the other to feel the discord of voices crying out for help? If we are, in fact, creatures made from the dust of the ground and made to be caretakers of the earth from within its nourishing bosom, the possibility is real. To establish this connection, I will turn to a biblical sketch of human being that is intimately tied to the trees.

The Tree of Life

One of the most notable images that we encounter in the Bible's opening account of creation is that of the Tree of Life, which sits at the center of creation (Gen 2:9). Both name and location were significant as both signified the opportunity for *homo divinus* to participate in the ordering of creation around the life-giving presence of God. Humanity was made to be gardeners, serving the rest of creation by orienting it around the Tree of Life, which brought with it the presence and promise of God unto life, rather than around the Tree of the Knowledge of Good and Evil, which would move creation towards death.[12]

The latter way was the choice for humanity to elevate itself, which could only be disastrous. After all, humanity's creation came from the dust of the ground, not from some place above. And the commission given to humanity was to tend to the garden—plants and animals. The name that Genesis gives to the first man is *Adam*, a play on words in Hebrew for the word for "dirt" or "earth." As biblical scholar Richard Bauckham explains, "The earthiness of humans signifies a kinship with the Earth itself and with other earthly creatures, plants and animals. Human life is embedded in the physical world with all that that implies of dependence on the natural systems of life."[13] God gives humanity a unique place, but that place is unique because of its commission, not because it made humanity separate

---

12. Note that in Gen 3:3, as the situation for creation begins to sour, Eve identifies the tree with forbidden fruit at the center of creation. The stage is set for her fall and Adam's to follow. As the caretakers enmeshed within creation and meant to organize creation around the life-giving presence of God, creation inevitably follows them into exile and death (Gen 3:17). Eve, who receives her name in 3:20 as "mother of the living", ironically begins the movement away from life. Adam, whose own name is a pun drawing upon his creation from the dirt of the earth (*adamah*), also ironically plunges the earth itself and her creatures into a state of separation from her life. Knowledge will abound with the new center, but life will slip away. The man of the dirt will himself dissolve back into the earth, removing any sign of the unique but fleeting life (3:19).

13. Bauckham, *Bible and Ecology*, 21.

in its daily life. Indeed, humanity needed (and still needs!) the fruit of the earth for growth and strength. The fact of that neediness was a good thing, bestowed by God as a gift that enabled recognition of the good that was all around them.[14] Humanity was to draw from the earth wisely in order to return to the earth to tend it. Humanity and the earth mutually presented "gifts" to each other, as Norman Wirzba puts it.[15]

Furthermore, while certainly endowed in special ways with a capacity to relate to one another, to order creation, and to build together, the most basic capacities of humanity were never meant to exceed those of the rest of creation. After all, humanity is not the fastest or the strongest creature on earth by a long shot and is outpaced in sight and hearing by many animals and in lifespan especially by the trees. Humanity's special abilities pertain to the ability to order creation with a wider view than the animals. Just as the trees often find themselves in competitive relationship in the forests, so do animals, rising in hostility toward each other as resources dwindle. Humanity, at least in capacity even if not always realized in practice, has the ability to attend to the earth in a way that is attentive to the needs of places and all of the creatures of those places. Historian William Cronon offers an example of this local attentiveness to the earth in his *Changes in the Land*. He describes a precolonial New England (as we know it) environment in which the indigenous peoples carefully attended to the habitat. They carefully burned brush, creating rich humus without endangering the forests themselves. In return, the now rich soil was able to sustain the varied agricultural practices of the people while providing nourishment for wild berries, which in turn invited deer to increase procreation. The positive effects were further felt by other animals in the food chain, from beavers to bears. The result was a landscape that left the would-be colonizers marveling at the plenty of the land, something that fairly quickly disappeared when they took over and enforced dominion that was not attentive to the place.[16] The precolonial environment benefited from a sort of creaturely "interdependence" that theologian Randy Woodley ascribes to the "intimacy" exhibited in Gen 2.[17]

14. See Wirzba, *This Sacred Life*.

15. Wirzba, *This Sacred Life*, 20.

16. Cronon, *Changes in the Land*, esp. 19–53.

17. Woodley, *Shalom and the Community of Creation*, 51. One such marker of intimacy that Woodley and others note is the practice of naming.

As a member of creation, the goal of humanity was to facilitate an "enmeshing," as Norman Wirzba describes it. This enmeshing recognizes the "entanglement" of life that reveals the interdependence of creatures. Just as Adam and Eve received their nourishment from every good fruit that the trees of the garden offered to them (Gen 2:29), so the trees too received their nourishment through the complex entanglement of biological creatures and functions in the soil that made home around the trees' roots, including human and animal waste. They also pulled life from the air that directly joined people and trees: as Adam and Eve breathed in the fresh oxygen exhaled by the trees, the leaves of the trees inhaled the carbon dioxide exhaled by people and animal. While only a brief sketch, we can see in this dynamic ecosystem an image of the sort of "meshwork" that contains creaturely life. In the perfect environment of the garden, we have a glimpse of the "meshwork" at its best: "Things can only be alive insofar as they *accept* and *flow within* fields of entanglement."[18] The harmony was possible because humanity—bearers of the divine image—lived amid the entanglement, receiving itself therein.

The enmeshing enabled humanity, if appropriately attentive, to order creation in a way that was uniquely attentive to the particularities of each member of creation. Just as involved parents are in a better position than strangers are to understand the uniqueness of their children and provide accordingly, God enmeshed the human image bearers within creation so that they could labor unto the good that each member needed. Distance would not do. They worked together, "cultivating" and "keeping" the garden (Gen 2:15). Their work was to extend in this way to all of the earth (Gen 1:28). In that setting prior to an accursed relationship to the earth (Gen 3:17–19) and prior to modern farm equipment and gardening tools, one can imagine the intimacy of their own hands enmeshed within the soil that they joyfully worked. Similarly, the intimacy extended to the animals, whom they knew well enough to name (Gen 2:19–20).

Ultimately, the work of ordering was to encircle all of creation—to extend the enmeshing to the whole earth—around that special tree that God made, in which he joined the life-giving fruit that offered daily nourishment with his life-giving word of promise that sustained life eternally. Humanity's task was to bring the fruit of the Tree of Life to a place of

---

18. Wirzba, *This Sacred Life*, 119 (emphasis his); though less developed, Elisabeth Moltmann-Wendel offers a similar theological reading of human personhood and the body. Moltmann-Wendel, *I Am My Body*, 47.

impact throughout the earth. In the words of Randy Woodley, the task was one of spreading the shalom of God.[19] While trees in general have a remarkable impact on the global ecosystem,[20] they can only have this impact if their roots are healthy. Their heart and brain can rightly be located in their root system. A damaged or hindered root system marks certain doom to trees. Shallow roots expose them to the toppling forces of windstorms in the summer and to hypothermia in the winter. Strong and deep roots sustain the life of the tree through the winter. They pull nitrogen from the soil, make alliances with ground fungi, provide for younger "daughter" trees, and communicate with neighboring trees over a wide range. The roots supply energy to the rest of the tree so that it can reach toward the sun's rays of light in order to create energizing sugar with the help of photosynthesis. In short, without the roots deeply embedded in the earth's soil, trees—and the earth with them—would be doomed. Strong roots enable the global impact of trees.

Should it be any surprise, then, that at the heart of the garden of Eden stood a tree with special roots? This tree bore even greater significance than the neighboring trees did. The neighboring trees bore fruit that was good for physical nourishment, enabling life. But the Tree of Life bore fruit that nourished unto eternal life (Gen 3:22–24). It is as though this one, special tree, the tree that bore the fruit of the promise of life from the lips of God, were a meeting place between the abode of God (heaven) and the home of his creation (earth). This special tree had two sets of roots, firmly establishing it in two worlds and joining those two worlds. Its double-rootedness made it the bearer of life in the fullest, both physically nourishing and sustaining God's creatures with his Word of life.

The hope of this divine commission remains long after the original image bearers were expelled from the garden. Even after the fall from grace, the image of the Tree of Life keeps emerging throughout Scripture, symbolizing the hope of renewed life to the fullest. The tree appears by name at least a couple of times. In Prov 3:18, finding and resting in the wisdom of God brings about at least an approximation of eating of the Tree of Life, for creation was made in the wisdom of God (3:19). At the end of John's confounding and tumultuous imagery in Revelation, we arrive at an image

19. Woodley sees "shalom" as tying together the biblical motifs of peace and active peacemaking in a way that "leans heavily into the concepts of love, justice, and [care for] God's created intention" for all creation. Woodley, *Shalom and the Community of Creation*, 10–11.

20. See Wohlleben, *Hidden Life of Trees*.

of the new earth, and it is once again encircled around the Tree of Life, here clearly identified alongside the divine throne (22:1–2).

This imagery in Revelation is especially interesting because of the way that it evokes the imagery of a tree full of life alongside a nourishing river—an image that echoes throughout Scripture. The river flows from the thrones of Father and Son, making it "living water" beyond the normal scope of living water, which otherwise referred to the running water of rivers and streams. The narrator identifies this special living water with the Holy Spirit (22:17; see also John 7:37–38), completing the triune imagery. The living Spirit-water then nourishes the Tree of Life, which then bears twelve kinds of fruit each month—likely an image for the twelve disciples and apostles, who were commissioned to take the good news of Jesus to the nations (cf. Rev 21:14), both Jews and gentiles (Rev 22:2), as well as the twelve tribes of Israel that were formed in the Old Covenant to be the means by which all of the nations would be blessed.[21] The tree also bears leaves that bring healing to all. Of course, all of these images have their root in Gen 2:10–17, where the narrator describes the river that waters the garden and the Tree that gives the fruit of life. The images continue to intertwine throughout the Old Testament. A new tree of peace emerging from the baptismal waters of the flood is implied in Gen 8:11, where the dove returns to Noah with a fresh olive leaf, signaling the return of dry land. In Ps 1:3, the one who delights in God's ways is like a tree "planted by streams of water" with leaves that do not wither. Jeremiah 17:8 says the same of those who trust in the Lord. The eschatological imagery of Ezek 47 multiplies the trees. Wherever the abundant river flows, trees will follow; their leaves will not wither, and they will bear fruit each month *for every living creature.*

The significance of trees, then, reverberates in the pages of Scripture, even to the point of divine appointment. More than markers, they are agents at the heart of God's creation sent to nourish and regulate it, and they are mirrors reflecting a lost paradise encircling a special double-rooted tree and

---

21. The imagery of a fresh crop each month is all the more meaningful when one considers subsistence living, as most cultures have practiced throughout the history of the earth. For instance, William Cronon describes a system among the former New England Indigenous peoples where each cycle of the moon (that is, each month) brought about a new way of gathering sustenance. They knew and named the cycles according to the ways that they had discerned for the season, from planting to harvesting to hunting of various animals, to name a few. Cronon, *Changes in the Land,* 37–43. The image of the new earth in Rev 22 presents the double-rooted Tree of Life that provides sustenance that is both physically and spiritually nourishing, and it does so anew each month. The creatures of earth will not need to look elsewhere for food of either sort—physical or spiritual.

a reconstituted paradise once again encircling perhaps many double-rooted trees. The health of trees signifies the health of the animate creatures of God, both animals and God's gardeners, who in turn labor unto the health of the earth itself, including its trees. The relationship is an enmeshing. One cannot truly speak of humanity apart from these giants that emerge from the land across the earth. They belong together. This context is crucial for beginning to understand the situatedness of humanity as people made to face God and to present the gift of a healthy creation to him. It is a context that begins to make sense of prayer. I have already suggested above that the trees themselves might well cry out to God in prayer and praise. The sketch on the importance of trees to the earth and in the biblical narrative should only strengthen the suggestion. My interest now shifts briefly to human prayer from within the earth and alongside its trees. Human prayer is at its most faithful when it is attuned to the cries of the earth, including her trees.

Prayer and the Breath of Life

At the outset, it is undeniable that human beings are embodied creatures. The most basic reality of human being begins with the fundamentally physical sexual act of parents wherein mother and father each contribute themselves to the formation of a new being that materially resembles each yet is identical to neither. We are physical beings who receive ourselves from other physical beings. Furthermore, beyond the point of conception, human beings grow through intimate physical connection with their mother, from whom they receive milk, and eventually more directly with the earth, from whom we receive nourishment after weaning. The basic physicality of our being is proper to who we are as human beings.[22]

Yet when it comes to prayer, Christians rarely consider the significance of physicality. We often emphasize closed eyes, shutting out the world, and we pray for abstract ideals or the application of abstract ideals. We want safety from harsh weather, healing from sickness, and provision of food. However, we rarely stop to consider that the means that we are asking for God to use in each of these situations depend upon horrible material histories. Our homes are mostly built on land that has been taken by violence and terraformed, destroying local ecosystems. For instance, American

---

22. See Moltmann-Wendel's insightful analysis of the goodness of human physicality and the way that Jesus seemed deliberately to play on this human reality, especially in Mark's Gospel account. Moltmann-Wendel, *I Am My Body*, 37, 44–45.

houses face the annual onslaught of mice who run free gathering food and procreating without many of their historic predators. These predators have a harder time surviving in American urban and suburban environments, and even in developed rural areas filled with fences. Thus, mice are free to grow in numbers, sometimes at a rate that grows out of control in the crawl spaces of houses.[23] Similarly, much of our modern medical advancement, from the development of vaccinations to advanced surgical procedures, have come at the expense of racialized human beings. The two great medical innovators were German scientists, who experimented upon Jewish people, and American researchers, who experimented upon African-Americans. Meanwhile, in contrast to the vast majority of cultures historically (though not all), the world's food supply is enmeshed in a complex global system of exploitation that preys upon the poor. A large number of bananas in American grocery stores come from poor Costa Rican plantations where people are exploited for American luxury. Pineapples come from Central America and the Philippines in similar exploitative networks.[24] Far from an attempt to invoke guilt, these examples should suffice to demonstrate the fissure between what we ask in our prayers and the material reality of exploitation in which we are enmeshed.

My purpose here, though, is not to dwell on the negative. Rather, I would like to recover the positive theological significance of human enmeshing within the earth, especially for prayer. At heart, prayer is creaturely utterance to God, a calling out from our material condition for God's intervention or for a show of praise from the peculiarities of our place.[25] It is the highly specific utterance of "attunement" to God's ways for those praying and for their places. As Brian Bantum describes it, "[p]rayer is the

23. On the environmental unsustainability of our global economy, especially as a dream sold to the world, see Ghosh, *Great Derangement*.

24. For historical studies that show the starvation of tens of millions globally in order to sustain rice and wheat imports in the modern Western world, see Davis, *Late Victorian Holocausts*; Mukerjee, *Churchill's Secret War*; for a summary of some of the atrocities enacted against the earth in some contemporary farming practices, such as in the production of potatoes, poultry, and beef, see Wirzba, *Food and Faith*, 58–67.

25. My use of "place" is meant to draw upon technical conversation that distinguishes between the generic notion of empty, meaningless space, and the formation of spaces in specific, enculturated ways that are full of meaning. The latter refers to "place" or "places." Places emerge through the enmeshing of real people living in real environments. As theologian John Inge puts it, "Places then develop their own story as a result of human experience in them." Inge, *Christian Theology of Place*, 124.

possibility of . . . transformation" of people shaped by and living within places.[26] Prayer belongs to places.

Nowhere is the locally embedded nature of prayer more evident than in consideration of the most basic fact of prayer: it presumes breath. In fact, all verbal communication takes breath for granted since it relies upon inhaling and exhaling, where the breath travels across the vocal cords and creates audible resonances. Verbal language is the organization of these noises. Prayer, in turn, is the direction of these material, breathy utterances towards God. In Christian confession, we specifically see these breathy utterances as communications in and by the Holy Spirit, who lifts prayer to the Father and sometimes even offers groans beyond our normal capacity or consciousness (Rom 8:26–27).

Perhaps unexpectedly, we encounter a confluence of our own breathy prayers and the Holy Spirit, for the Spirit's self is described by Scripture to be the Breath of God. In fact, the word for "breath" in both Hebrew and Greek—the languages of the Bible—is the same as the word for "Spirit" and "wind." The Bible often deliberately plays on this verbal interchange, linking the breath by which we live, the Holy Spirit that brings fuller life, and the wind that moves.[27] For instance, in Ps 104:29–30, English translations relay that when humanity gives up its breath, it dies, whereas when it receives the Holy Spirit, it lives. Noting the play on words, though, we quickly realize that the distinction in the psalm is between the arrival of death with one's final exhale and the renewal of life with each breath that we take. Psalm 104 heightens this basic reality by showing the qualitatively higher life that accompanies God's Holy Breath. The passage alludes to Gen 2 by pointing out that God's Holy Breath does not merely offer another opportunity to inhale among the hundreds of millions that the average person takes in a lifetime. This unique Breath, the Holy Breath of God, *creates*, just as it did in Gen 2. As if the allusion were not strong enough, the psalmist clarifies: "and you renew the face of the ground." The creature made from the soil of the ground received life originally through God's Holy Breath. The psalmist declares the renewal of the same possibility: inhaling God's Holy Breath gives new life to the creatures formed from the earth.

26. Bantum, *Redeeming Mulatto*, 181.

27. Averbeck, "Holy Spirit in the Hebrew Bible," 23; see also Averbeck, "Breathe, Wind, and the Holy Spirit," 37. Here Averbeck concludes that "[w]e could even talk about these practices as the way the human spirit 'breathes' in and out (inhaling and exhaling) the 'breath' of the Spirit of God."

The Psalms provide an excellent opportunity to play with the full range of nuance in words, for they present the heart of the Bible's poetic tradition. Poetry, says Owen Barfield, is able to play in multiple fields of meaning at once because at its best it is a use of language that reaches back to an older, higher form of language. *Poetic diction*, he says, takes "connections which are now apprehended as metaphor" and seeks to recover a time and place where they "were once perceived as immediate realities."[28] In this earlier, higher language, Barfield posits a poetic form that is proper to speech and is able to say more than our contemporary prosaic uses of words. For example, when my child says, "Papa," she means something very specific. She is referring to me and knows me to be her father. "Papa" is a unique title that she has for me, but she also knows that her "Dada" is my "Papa." Prose moves increasingly toward specificity, and the word "Papa" demonstrates the specificity by giving my daughter a narrow focus, as opposed to any other "man" or "guy." Conversely, when my friend's child says, "Papa," he means both something specific and something general. He calls me and his father by that name. However, it would be a mistake to assume that he sees no distinction between us. In addition to the physical differences in our appearances, he *knows* us in different ways. Even when he keeps calling me "Papa," at no point does he ascribe to me the loftiness of relationship that he does to his father or that my daughter does to me. Barfield argues that my friend's child "has one single meaning, 'papa,' but it is a meaning which contains within itself the capacity to split up, or unfold or evolve into two separate ideas, 'Father' and 'man', of which one is more particular."[29] It is not that the child consciously thinks of one word with multiple meanings; rather "Papa" is able to bear a larger field in poetic diction while holding onto differences in the world of perception. Poets thrive on using words fluidly in this way, evoking in their hearers and readers multiple senses, referents, and feelings all at once, often playing them off each other.

Arguably, the Bible does precisely this. Think, for instance, of all that is contained in the Gen 1 refrains, "Let there be." Each day contains a new command that seemingly brings forth much more than the words "light" or "water" or "dry land" might otherwise be able to. God's poetic speech is able to do infinitely more than the speech of creatures, but by analogy, human poetic diction does something similar. In the Bible, a perfect example is the frequent interchangeability of breath/spirit/wind to say more within a single

28. Barfield, *Poetic Diction*, 85.

29. Barfield, *Poetic Diction*, 74n4.

context. In addition to Ps 104, other passages also exhibit this tendency. In Gen 1:2, the Spirit/Breath of God "hovers over the deep," while a chapter later, God forms humanity out of the soil of the earth and then *breathes* into his nostrils giving him life, which could also be read as sending his *Spirit* to animate the clay molding. Jesus picks up on this precise play on words in John 20:22. After bypassing the disciples' locked door, he then "breathed on them and said, 'Receive the Holy Spirit,'" alluding to Gen 2 while highlighting the play on words. At Pentecost in Acts 2, the Spirit enters the room as a strong wind and empowers the same disciples (2:2–4).[30] Later in Acts, the narrator appeals to the poetic possibilities of wind/Spirit while seemingly alluding to Jonah's travails aboard a ship in the Mediterranean Sea. After fighting for some time with a strong wind on the sea, in 27:15, the crew members finally give way to being "driven along" with it.

The special importance for our purposes here is to consider the place of the Breath of God in prayer. As noted above, breath is the precondition of our prayer, for it both enables the life of the praying one and creates the possibility of speech that can become prayer. Breath is basic to life as we know it, and it sustains all of God's creatures on earth. Poetically, it points to a fuller life, one that lies behind in paradise lost where the Breath of God passed between Tree of Life and all other creatures. It also points forward to the fullness of life renewed with the new Tree of Life, nourished in the Breath of God and sending out that same Breath so that all might inhale and live in the fullest. Even in our current situation, creation bears the mark of anticipation, enabling God's creatures to call out to him. Breath ties together God's animate creatures and the trees. The air that we breathe that is proper to natural life is able to sustain humanity and the animals because of its richness in oxygen, and that richness is a direct result of the work of trees. According to Peter Wohlleben, trees really do "inhale" the carbon dioxide that we exhale, and they really do "exhale" the oxygen that we inhale. He points out that while trees cease exhaling oxygen after the sun sets, "a steady movement of air through the

---

30. Willie James Jennings adds that the nuance of wind at Pentecost carries the sense of that which is uncontrollable by we creatures. *Acts*, 27–28. The Holy Breath of God animates the apostles as they inhale God's Breath even as the same Breath of God moves in a way that they cannot control. The repeated use of the same words throughout the biblical narrative in a way that fluidly moves through all of these meanings—Spirit, breath, wind—allows the possibility of recapturing what Barfield calls poetic diction, which can communicate the whole range of nuances at once, allowing them to be unified in order to paint a fuller picture than each nuance could otherwise do by itself.

forest ensures that all the gases are well mixed at all times."[31] That is to say, a steady *wind* ensures the movement of the oxygen through the trees and beyond so that we might *breathe* in its life.[32]

Imagine, poetically, the beautiful *theological* tale of life enabled and sustained by the enmeshing of humanity, soil, wind, breath, and trees. Imagine the significance of Scripture's joining together people and the earth, breath and the Holy Spirit, and the Tree of Life and the special nourishing that comes from God. The confluence of all these things testifies to the need for humanity to be enmeshed, ultimately with God. Thanks to God's beautiful design, this enmeshing takes place amid the enmeshing of humanity and the earth. They speak, too, to the need to attend to our location as creatures within the earth *calling out to God in his Holy Breath*. Prayer does not exist apart from our place in the earth.

God provided original creation—and will provide again in new creation—as the setting for his life-giving presence. It is the trees that cycle the life-giving breath of the earth. How much greater is the life that comes from breathing in the very breath of God—the Spirit of life—which cycles in and out of the Tree of Life. Consider, too, the use of "tree" to refer to the paradoxically crafted cross that brought not only death but an agonizing one at that! Acts speaks of the Christ who hung from the "tree" (5:30; 10:39[33]). Jesus redeemed even those sadly mutilated pieces of wood that turned a life-giving tree into a device of torture and death, enabling the hope of life through it. All of creation looks forward to the renewal as the one who redeemed it hung on the tree and expelled his breath, sending it forth for us to inhale. Because he breathed out his Spirit-breath, we may now inhale that same Spirit-breath. The inhale becomes the precondition of our prayer: we utter our cries to God already in dependence upon the Spirit-God who is our breath of life! Our prayer, then, anticipates the new creation, when all the earth will be permeated by the life-giving Spirit-breath of God with the new and fully-redeemed Tree of Life at the center, nourishing all of creation once again. Our prayer is eschatological, looking

31. Wohlleben, *Hidden Life of Trees*, 224.

32. As Bessel van der Kolk points out, this breath that is the precondition for life itself is also key in ensuring our quality of life. Healthy breathing begets healthy heart function. Additionally, "the way one breathes can improve problems with anger, depression, and anxiety." He has successfully used techniques of attentiveness to the breath to treat patients with severe degrees of PTSD. Van der Kolk, *Body Keeps the Score*, 270–71.

33. The NIV translations of these passages refer to Christ's death on a "cross," but the Greek word is actually ξυλον, meaning "tree."

forward to the end that is not a removal from the earth but rather a renewal of all the earth, along with the creatures that she has been given to nourish. Whether consciously or not, our prayer takes place from within the earth and, therefore, ought to be for the good of the earth.

Concluding Thoughts: Needy Prayer in the Earth

As I have argued, the reality of human existence has the precondition of the earth and of the breath that ties us to the towering trees of the earth. Prayer shares the same preconditions. Prayer should take shape amid awareness of our place and its needs. Even the prayer of praise takes for granted our material conditions within the earth that elicit the mood of praise. Yet too often, our prayers find themselves sealed off from our material setting. As noted above, we pray for good things: shelter, health, and provision. However, in the hopes of having our needs met, we are rarely attentive to the injustices that have gone into the making of the places in which we live and the processes that our places presume. We pray without attention to the structures in which we are embedded, for better and for worse. Our prayers can then come at the expense of others—people, animals, and the earth itself.

We are joined in the earth, and we depend upon the earth and each other through our places in the earth. This reality itself reflects the reality of our dependence upon God, who created humanity as symbiotic members of his holy garden encircling the divine presence manifest through a tree. Our joyful neediness was to transpire within the trust that God's life-giving presence and promise of life could sustain us through trust in the processes of creation in which he placed us. Trusting God was trusting him to gift life within the boundaries that he established. Trusting God was trusting that his limits enabled flourishing, not anxiety (Matt 6:26–31). It was only in turning away from trust that God could and would provide fullness through the natural setting in which he established *all* of his creatures that creation began to experience its deterioration from its harmony. Humanity came from the dirt of the earth, and all the earth fell with the disobedience of the people of the dirt. Humanity exhibited the desire to shape *all* of creation around human superiority and self-sufficiency: after all, if you eat of the forbidden tree, the serpent said, "you will be like God" (Gen 3:5). But self-sufficiency was never supposed to be the point. Humanity was supposed to embrace its limits and thrive in enmeshed dependence upon God and his earth. That is what it means to be creatures: we depend upon others and especially upon God. As Norman Wirzba wisely observes, ignoring our limits brings about "abuse" and "is degrading or sacrilegious."[34]

Prayer is a return to this posture of dependence. It is an embrace of neediness and the needs of fellow creatures—human and otherwise. At its best, prayer turns to God from a position of openness to the needs all around and everywhere. This kind of prayer wants the best for *all* of creation. It seeks God's kingdom come "*on earth* as it is in heaven" (Matt 6:10). It seeks a kingdom that thrives because it is needy and that reaches out to God in dependence in a way that joins in the chorus of voices through creation singing and crying out to God. In his *Canticle of the Sun*, Saint Francis embedded his own prayer within the prayers resounding throughout creation. Each stanza begins with his prayer and praise and then moves quickly to a call for the sun, the moon, the wind, and the trees—among many others— to praise God. Saint Francis understood that humanity did not and should not live alone. It was good to be together with fellow humanity and with the animals and earth upon whom we daily depend. "Praise be You, my Lord, through our Sister Mother Earth / who sustains and governs us, / and who produces varied fruits with colored flowers and herbs."[35]

Bibliography

Averbeck, Richard. "Breathe, Wind, and the Holy Spirit in the Old Testament." In *Presence, Power, and Promise: The Role of the Spirit of God in the Old Testament*, edited by David G. Firth and Paul D. Wegner, 25–37. Downers Grove, IL: InterVarsity, 2011.

———. "The Holy Spirit in the Hebrew Bible and Its Connections to the New Testament." In *Who's Afraid of the Holy Spirit?*, edited by M. James Sawyer and Daniel B. Wallace, 15–36. Dallas, TX: Biblical Studies Press, 2005.

Bantum, Brian. *Redeeming Mulatto: A Theology of Race and Christian Hybridity.* Baylor University Press, 2016.

Barfield, Owen. *Poetic Diction: A Study in Meaning.* Oxford: Barfield, 2010.

Bauckham, Richard. *The Bible and Ecology: Rediscovering the Community of Creation.* Waco, TX: Baylor University Press, 2010.

Cronon, William. *Changes in the Land: Indians, Colonists, and the Ecology of New England.* 20th anniversary ed. New York: Hill and Wang, 2003.

Davis, Mike. *Late Victorian Holocausts: El Niño Famines and the Making of the Third World.* London: Verso, 2001.

34. Wirzba, *This Sacred Life*, 190.

35. Francis of Assisi, "Canticle of Brother Sun," §§3, 9.

Francis of Assisi. "The Canticle of Brother Sun." In *Readings in Western Religious Thought: II. The Middle Ages through the Reformation*, edited by Patrick V. Reid, translated by Regis J. Armstrong, 230–31. New York: Paulist, 1995.

Ghosh, Amitav. *The Great Derangement: Climate Change and the Unthinkable*. Chicago: University of Chicago Press, 2017.

Inge, John. *A Christian Theology of Place*. Aldershot, UK: Routledge, 2003.

Jennings, Willie James. *Acts: A Theological Commentary on the Bible*. Louisville, KY: Westminster John Knox, 2017.

Kimmerer, Robin Wall. *Braiding Sweetgrass: Indigenous Wisdom, Scientific Knowledge and the Teachings of Plants*. Minneapolis: Milkweed, 2013.

Moltmann-Wendel, Elisabeth. *I Am My Body: A Theology of Embodiment*. Translated by John Bowden. New York: Continuum, 1995.

Mukerjee, Madhusree. *Churchill's Secret War: The British Empire and the Ravaging of India during World War II*. New York: Basic, 2010.

Tolkien, J. R. R. "On Fairy-Stories." In *The Monsters and the Critics and Other Essays*, edited by Christopher Tolkien, 109–61. London: HarperCollins, 2006.

Van der Kolk, Bessel. *The Body Keeps the Score: Brain, Mind, and Body in the Healing of Trauma*. 2014. Reprint, New York: Penguin, 2015.

Wirzba, Norman. *Food and Faith: A Theology of Eating*. 2nd ed. New York: Cambridge University Press, 2019.

———. *This Sacred Life*. New York: Cambridge University Press, 2021.

Wohlleben, Peter. *The Hidden Life of Trees: What They Feel, How They Communicate—Discoveries from a Secret World*. Edited by Jane Billinghurst. Vancouver: Greystone, 2016.

Woodley, Randy. *Shalom and the Community of Creation: An Indigenous Vision*. Grand Rapids, MI: Eerdmans, 2012.

Tuvoye—"Let Us Pray"

By STEPHANIE LOWERY, PHD

It is also hoped that those Christians whose hearts are united with us in desire for this new enduement of power but who cannot be present, will send us a salutation and greeting by letter, that there may be a concert of prayer with them throughout the land during these days of waiting.

—D. L. MOODY

Introduction

FOR NEARLY TWENTY YEARS, I have been granted the opportunity to live in Kenya, a beautiful country with forty-four ethnic groups, each possessing their own language. *Tuvoye* is from the Kikamba language in Kenya, and simply translates as "Let us pray." Among the few Kikamba words which I have learned so far, this was one of the easiest to grasp, as the physical response to this phrase (bowing of heads and folding of hands) clearly demonstrates the meaning of the word. When worshipping in a church using Kikamba, I can at least understand when we are entering a time of prayer!

In the Kenyan context, prayer is taken with great seriousness. Several denominations—including my own, the Africa Inland Church—will often hold an all-night prayer vigil—referred to as a *kesha* in Swahili. The power of a prayer to bring down judgment or blessing is rarely doubted. This is true in Christianity; prayer is also perceived as powerful in Islam and African traditional religions (ATRs), the two other major religious traditions of Kenya.

I also write keeping in mind a friend who grew up in the church, but is now an ardent atheist, convinced that all religions are delusions. He

117

particularly detests when people say, "Sending thoughts and prayers!" in response to a hardship. Aside from his conviction that God does not exist, two of his key objections to this phrase are that, first, it seems to be used to excuse the person praying from any further action, and second, if the prayer is not answered with a "yes," it implies God is refusing to help.

My own experiences with prayer have been mixed—from times when it felt like my prayers went nowhere, to times when prayer brought clarity and closeness to Christ. I can also testify to a time when I miraculously received physical healing the day before a surgical procedure. Why is it that experiences of prayer can differ so greatly from one occasion to the next? What are we to think about the effectiveness of prayer?

Perhaps more than any other act, prayer highlights the limits of our comprehension of the God of Scripture. Prayer holds together what some may mistakenly perceive as paradoxes: God is immeasurably greater than his creation yet stoops to listen to the cries and whispers of our hearts. He is faithful and unchanging, yet nevertheless chooses to respond to and work through the prayers of imperfect, limit human beings. Through prayer, our own hearts are revealed.

Listening to a variety of perspectives has pushed me to reflect more on the purposes of prayer from a Christian perspective. One of the first questions is, what *are* the goals of prayer? The Bible shows us a wide range of prayer types—praising and requesting, for instance—as we see clearly in the book of Psalms. Prayer can also take a variety of forms, from song and dance, to loud appeal in communal worship, to inward heart cries, or symbolic actions such as lighting a candle or prostrating oneself on the floor. But amongst its various types and forms, is there any common thread? There are at least two key goals in Christian prayer: communion and communication with the Triune God.[1]

Communion

In speaking of prayer as communion, I mean that one goal of prayer ought to be to draw closer to the God of the Bible: to grow more intimate in one's relationship with God. Aylward Shorter describes prayer as the basis for worship and the essential disposition in a religious person.[2] Tite Tiénou affirms that "right theology begins, continues and ends with right

1. Shorter, *Prayer in the Religious Traditions*, 2–3.
2. Shorter, *Prayer in the Religious Traditions*, 2.

prayer," highlighting the centrality of prayer in worship and in thinking through our beliefs.[3] Further, praying demonstrates a desire for fellowship with God. At the same time, to pray is to take the risk of willingly opening ourselves to God.[4]

A desire to learn about non-Christian beliefs—in my context, African traditional religions (ATRs)—has further impacted my view of Christian prayer as communion. Aylward Shorter's study of ATRs describes a wide range of perspectives on God, sometimes referred to as the Supreme Being. Many ATRs believe in numerous divinities and spirit beings who can receive prayers. Also, most ATRs have no doubt about God's existence but vary in their perspective of how involved he is in daily life. If God is regularly experienced in one's daily life, he is more likely to be prayed to. However, if a particular ATR views the Supreme Being as more remote from his creation, then prayers may be directed to ancestral spirits or lesser divinities.[5]

There is also the possibility of religion where the Supreme Being is believed to exist but is hostile or ambivalent towards his creation; in that case, he may be dreaded, rather than approached like the loving, caring Father of the Lord's Prayer. For example, the Duruma ethnic group of Kenya have traditionally held the view that God created the world, but that human beings are created as expendable in God's sight. They are not loved for who they are nor do they have an intrinsic value. Likewise, Aylward Shorter records multiple occurrences of the Dinka people of Sudan referring to themselves as "ants" before God, which Shorter interprets as humiliating themselves before God.[6] Clearly a person's view of God will have a direct impact on their desire for a close relationship with God.

Seeking Closer Communion with the Triune God

Whether or not a person desires communion with God depends greatly on what they believe about God's character. In other words, if you believe God is generally angry and vengeful, or capricious, or uncaring of your daily struggles, you are less likely to pray or long for closer fellowship with God.

3. Tiénou, "Lessons from the Prayer Habits," 268–71.

4. Magesa, *What Is Not Sacred?*, 65.

5. Shorter, *Prayer in the Religious Traditions*, 10–12.

6. Shorter, *Prayer in the Religious Traditions*, 47, 88–89, 130.

Likewise, if you believe God is unable to deliver you, why bother praying to him, or what confidence can you have when you do pray?

Likewise, if a Christian has a greatly skewed view of the God of Scripture, they may find it difficult to pray. For instance, if I think God is angry with me, constantly watching to catch all of my mistakes, I may develop an attitude of resentment or fear toward God, and thus find it hard to pray. The wrong perception of God is bound to affect my prayer life, among other areas of my faith walk.

Tiénou notes that in ATRs, God is often viewed as a "dependable" and "natural ally" of humans, which then explains why prayers in an African context often "expect God to comply with [their] wishes."[7] This is not just an ATR view of prayer; it exists in Western contexts when God is viewed as a Santa figure, whose sole purpose in life is to give out pleasant gifts. Some preachers wrongly teach that when a Christian prays in faith, God is bound to provide whatever they request, which turns prayer into an infallible delivery service. These warped views of prayer reflect a deficient theology, and sadly miss the point that Christian prayer is a gift, welcoming us into the presence of the holy and loving God whom we can call our Father, as the beginning of the Lord's Prayer highlights.

However, there are times when non-Christians pray and a Christian will find that the content of that prayer is one which she can agree with and repeat in her own prayers. For example, the Susu ethnic group of Guinea have a ritual prayer that is offered by young men before his "trial of courage," which requires him to kill a leopard: "Father, O mighty force, that force which is in everything, come down between us, fill us, until we be like thee, until we be like thee."[8] Christians pray to Jesus, whereas the Susu traditionally did not, so the God to whom Christians direct their prayers is not the same. However, as a Christian, this prayer reminds me that God is present in all places. It also speaks eloquently to what the New Testament teaches: in Christ, God has "come down" to live among us, and he does send his Spirit to live in us and make us like him. This non-Christian prayer reminds me of the wonder of the gospel, and of the truth that one goal of prayer is to draw closer to God. As I draw closer, as I spend more time in his presence, my hope is that I will indeed come to resemble him more and more.

7. Tiénou, "Lessons from the Prayer Habits," 269.

8. Shorter, *Prayer in the Religious Traditions*, 33.

With sincerity and hope, the believer who, like the psalmist, has been overwhelmed by God's greatness, goodness and love can pray, "As the deer pants for streams of water, so my soul pants for you, my God" (Ps 42:1), or, "You, God, are my God, earnestly I seek you; I thirst for you, my whole being longs for you, in a dry and parched land where there is no water. I have seen you in the sanctuary and beheld your power and your glory. Because your love is better than life, my lips will glorify you" (Ps 63:1–3). Prayer is not just about bringing our requests to God; in prayer we spend time with God, even when that includes silence.

This resonates with South African Anglican archbishop Desmond Tutu's description of the relationship with God as "a love affair and ultimately the greatest joy is just to be with the Beloved, to drink in the beauty of the Beloved in a silence that will become ever more wordless and imageless—the silence of just being together. . . . We seek to give ourselves to the One who first gave himself to us, this eternally self-giving and self-emptying kenotic One. May God grant that we will all grow in that intimacy that enables us to know we are loved with a love that will never let us go."[9] For Christians, prayer is a great gift precisely because of the wholly loving and good God who welcomes us into his presence; because of God's nature, prayer for the Christian is not an empty ritual, not merely a duty, but a blessing.

Tutu encourages the praying person that "as we keep still in the presence of God, we luxuriate in this knowledge: that we are loved, that all we are, all we have is a gift, freely and generously bestowed. All we must do is to be deeply thankful, to be eucharistic people, to say forever: 'Thank you, God, for loving me so much.'"[10] Since God is a loving heavenly father, we are welcome to come to him purely to be in his presence, even if we do not know what or how to pray at that moment. Thankfully, we are encouraged that in the times when we feel unable to pray, the Spirit is praying on our behalf (Rom 8:26).

Again, for some Christians developing a robust prayer life is a struggle precisely because of their distorted view of God: to them, God is seemingly distant or difficult to approach. Practically speaking, I find it helpful to immerse myself in Scripture, so that I am constantly reminded of God's abundant acts of goodness to his people. As I hear these truths

9. Tutu, *African Prayer Book*, xvii.

10. Tutu, *African Prayer Book*, xviii–xix.

over and over, they become "louder" than the lie that God does not truly want to hear about my struggles.

Sometimes prayer is our last resort, and that too is revealing of our heart. As Peskett notes, prayer "reveals where our true confidence lies."[11] A person might try other means of meeting their need before turning to prayer as a last resort, specifically because they actually have more confidence in their own ability to "fix" the situation than in God's desire to do so. The lack of prayer in the Christian's life indicates a deeper problem, and a distance from God.

For Tanzanian Laurenti Magesa, prayer is a way of life or orientation that shapes a person's view of the world.[12] Prayer alters and purifies the person praying, as well as indicating that the pray-er seeks to see God at work in their experiences.[13] We could say that prayer indicates our desire to see with eyes of faith, so that we can perceive God; it is a longing to realize where God is at work in our midst. It is a longing to see God at work around us and in us. Tutu reminds the praying person that prayer can "help you to become ever more and more fully what you already are: a child of God, known by name and whose very hairs are numbered."[14] When prayer is a person's way of life, they are alert for signs of God's presence and work; we could say that a praying person keeps their eyes on Christ, which gives them a clearer view of the world around them as they are enabled by the Spirit to see God's world rightly. Prayer is transformative. North African theologian Saint Augustine once prayed, "O love ever burning and never extinguished charity, My God set me on fire."[15] Quite right—may the Refining Fire purify us that we may become in reality what God has declared us to be: holy and made in his own image!

Consequences of Communion with God

As mentioned, spending time with God is transformative. One consequence of opening ourselves to God is that we will find our own perspectives on life altered and enlarged.[16] For instance, in 2 Kgs 6 Elisha and his servant

11. Peskett, "Prayer in the Old Testament," 23.

12. Magesa, *What Is Not Sacred?*, 66.

13. Magesa, *What Is Not Sacred?*, 66.

14. Tutu, *African Prayer Book*, xx.

15. Tutu, *African Prayer Book*, 10.

16. Shorter, *Prayer in the Religious Traditions*, 4.

awake one morning to find the city of Dothan besieged by the Aramean army. While his servant fell into despair and fear, as many would do, Elisha had a different view of their situation. The prophet was fully aware of the army surrounding Dothan but possessed some insight or confidence that his servant lacked: Elisha was confident that those with them are "greater" than the army besieging the city. Moreover, his confidence was not based on any human army that could come to Dothan's aid; rather, he had been given the spiritual eyes to see that the hills around them were full of a heavenly army, an army with horses and chariots of fire. It does indeed require the Spirit to enable us to see spiritual realities, and so Elisha's prayer was that God will allow the servant too to see the truth that is all around him: God is in control. God fulfills Elisha's request, and the change in perspective is immediate. Like scales falling from his eyes, the servant suddenly sees what had been true all along: God's heavenly army are present and active. There is no reason to fear. Elisha's intimacy with his God shines forth quite clearly in this chapter. His prayers for deliverance and for judgment were answered with a "yes," and he certainly had knowledge and perspective granted by God.

What we see of Elisha in just this one chapter calls to mind Jesus's words in John 15:7, where Jesus urges the disciples to abide in him and have his words abiding in them. When this mutual abiding happens, the disciples will bear fruit, and what they pray for will happen! Jesus's own life reveals his intimacy with his Father, an intimacy maintained by his habit of regular withdrawal for prayer. Prayer is intended to attune us to God's voice, God's will, God's character. It is an opportunity to grow in knowledge and love of our Father.

We recall that Magesa views prayer as a lifestyle: his perspective is holistic, refusing to separate the spiritual from the more mundane aspects of life. Therefore, he sees spirituality and morality as being two sides of the same coin.[17] Here is what that looks like: as I pray and experience the love of God, I will in turn be filled with God's love and show that love to my neighbor in righteous words and deeds. So, for Magesa, prayer should transform a person inwardly and outwardly, in actions to those around them.

That being said, the transformation wrought through prayer can be painful, even when we can grasp and trust that the end result will truly be beneficial to us. As the world endures the current COVID pandemic, Christians, like Job, may find themselves full of questions about why God is allowing this situation. And like Job, we may find that even

17. Magesa, *What Is Not Sacred?*, 112.

after wrestling with this question—and God—we do not get the clarification we would desire. Instead, God brings to mind the many ways he has proved faithful in the past, and so urges us to continue trusting, but may not grant us insight into the "why" of the trial. In other words, God wants us to have faith that even when we don't understand his ways, we can trust his character and cling to him.

From personal example, I can keenly remember a prayer I prayed when I was in eighth grade. I had become a Christian at a young age but had realized that I was "coasting" in my faith, going through the motions but not making much effort to grow. The afternoon when that realization hit me, I prayed that God would help me to grow in my faith. Just a few months later, my father was diagnosed with cancer. We quickly travelled to the United States for treatment, and he was declared cancer-free, with 95 percent chance that the cancer would never return. We rejoiced and returned to Kenya two days after Christmas. But in less than six months, the cancer had returned, and the doctors advised an immediate return to the US. In twenty-four hours, we packed up my things from boarding school, packed some clothes at our home, and got on a flight back to the US, not knowing what was next or where we would live.

My dad spent the next two and a half years fighting cancer. I spent a lot of time struggling, feeling like I was wrestling with God, like Jacob. I prayed for healing, whether through the doctor's hands, chemotherapy, or miraculous means. Friends around the world also prayed for my dad. Yet while praying, I could find myself doubting God's goodness and feeling angry that he had not prevented the cancer. Why would God allow such a thing to happen to my dad? Some friends advised that I pray harder and have more faith, and my dad would be healed. Others reminded me of Rom 8:28–29, telling me that all things work to the good for those who love God and are called by him. I felt lost; I did not see how this cancer was working for good. And then my dad died a week before I started my last year in secondary school. Can I tell you, I really started to dislike Rom 8:28? When people quoted it to me, it felt like they were slapping me in the face. It took me years before I heard a sermon that helped me to understand that verse, and to indeed see some ways that God brought good out of that situation.

That was now over twenty years ago; I still do not understand why God allowed my father to get cancer in the first place, just like Job was never told why he went through his trials. Could God have prevented it? Yes. Could he have healed my father of the cancer, after allowing it? Yes

. . . but he chose not to do that. Instead, my father died in his mid-forties, his life and ministry overseas "cut short," from a human perspective. What happened to my prayers?

God eventually enabled me to see that Rom 8:28 says all things work together for good, meaning anything can be used for a good result in the life of the Christian. That does not mean that I must call the situation good. Cancer is terrible; I believe God hates it. It could not have existed before sin entered this world, and when Christ returns, it *will* be destroyed. But God is so great, powerful, and good that he can use *anything* to accomplish his purposes, even cancer. That cancer and pandemics and oppression exist grieves God's heart. At the same time, I do believe he heard my prayers. The prayer for healing was answered with a "no," but that time spent wrestling was indeed rewarded. The prayer for spiritual growth received a "yes," though I did not perceive that until later.

I had for quite some time misunderstood Rom 8:28. But if I had simply grasped the following verse, I would have seen at least one good God wanted to bring about in my life in answer to that prayer from eighth grade. Romans 8:29 explains, "For those whom [God] foreknew he also predestined to be conformed to the image of his Son, in order that he might be the firstborn among many brothers." God's desire is that his adopted children will gradually be transformed into the image of Christ himself. *That* is the good God has planned for each Christian! To reach that goal of Christlikeness requires some purification and pain. But my spiritual eyes were closed to that truth for quite some time.

As for me, I began studying the Bible and theology more seriously when I was facing great doubts and struggles in my own life. My prayers brought me closer to God. I learned more about God's character and learned to hold onto him. Through that hardship, I drew closer to God. I grew in my faith and my understanding of God; he gave me the gift of his presence in answer to my cries.

Communication

Prayer is communion and communication. However, even this statement needs to be unpacked. Just what do we communicate to God, and he to us? For one example, a person presenting their needs to God in prayer signals that the person has a need that they cannot meet in their own ability. As John S. Mbiti puts it when analyzing a Burundian and Rwandan prayer for offspring, "The human is presented here at the edge of his/her powers. So, the speaker becomes humble before God with honor, love, respect and obedience."[18] In prayer, we acknowledge our own limits and turn to God for help, in the belief that he is able to do all that we cannot. As Mbiti puts it, "God is the God of help, the final point of appeal."[19]

Yet we know that God says "no" to our requests at times. There are many reasons God may choose to respond this way to our prayers, or even ignore them, though we will not dwell long on this matter. For instance, if we refuse to turn from our sins, that refusal causes our prayers to be unacceptable and unheard by God. Howard Peskett makes the point that prayer is never intended to be an excuse or an escape for God's people, nor should we assume that he is pleased to hear all of our prayers. Peskett reminds the Christian that

> Sometimes *action* is needed: "The Lord said to Moses, 'Why are you crying out to me? Tell the Israelites to move on. Raise your hand . . . divide the sea . . .'" (Exodus 14,15 [*sic*]) Sometimes *sin must be dealt with*. When Joshua was flat on his face after the Israelites' defeat at Ai, the Lord said, "Stand up! What are you doing on your face? Israel has sinned . . ." (Joshua 7:6 . . .).
>
> *Prudence* may also be required: Nehemiah reports, "We prayed to our God and posted a guard day and night . . ." (Nehemiah 4:9). *Disobedience* will make God deaf (Proverbs 28:9). Of a disobedient people the Lord said, "When I called, they did not listen, so when they called, I would not listen" (Zechariah 7:13). *Injustices* must be corrected . . . (Isa. 58:6–11).[20]

God may deny a request because of sin or our failure to act. This highlights the necessity of confession, that we may be restored to fellowship with God. In some Christian circles, the acronym ACTS is used to elaborate various components of prayer: adoration, confession, thanksgiving, and supplication. Unfortunately, this acronym focuses on what we say to God, but makes no mention of the need for our silence in order to listen for God's response.

As Peskett says, prayer is not an excuse for inaction on the part of the one praying. Prayer is an action in itself and can be used by God to stir his people up to further action. At a pivotal moment in South Africa,

18. Mbiti, "*Kwambaza*," 16.

19. Mbiti, "*Kwambaza*," 16.

20. Peskett, "Prayer in the Old Testament," 23–24.

when the country's government claimed to be Christian but were not dismantling the cruel, unjust apartheid system, a group of theologians issued a call to prayer. Their document, entitled "A Theological Rationale and a Call to Prayer for the End to Unjust Rule" was a call to the church. The concern was that while the South African Council of Churches had in 1948 condemned apartheid as heresy, nothing had been done to translate these objections into action.[21] The "theological rationale" was calling for churches to pray about the situation and seek peaceful means of change, instead of just verbally condemning apartheid.

South African Villa-Vicencio argues that false piety treats prayer as an escape from political responsibility, while the Bible knows no gap "between prayer and social engagement."[22] Preaching about the problem, South African Allan A. Boesak concludes, "To pray does not mean that I will now fold my hands and close my eyes and sit back and let God do all the work. To pray means that I will say to God, 'I am now at your disposal. Use me, use me for peace, use me for justice, use me for compassion, use me for mercy, use me for love, use me for liberation so that your people can see and believe.'"[23] In prayer, we are to submit to God and offer to act as he directs, similar to Isaiah: "Here am I. Send me!" (Isa 6:8).

It would also be reductionistic to view our communication with God as limited to requests that we make. Unfortunately, we can easily fall into the trap of thinking this way. Shorter observes that in ATRs, the belief is that "prayer, if it is properly conducted and recited in all its details, must produce an infallible effect, is also quite common. If there is no answer to prayer, it is felt that there must be a mistake somewhere."[24] Tiénou too notes that traditional Africa religions would largely define prayer as asking and petitioning. Therefore, it should not be surprising that this perspective is carried over into Christianity when one converts from ATR, and "the assurance of efficacious prayers may be one of the motivations for joining the various Christian groups in Africa."[25] The ATR view of prayer in this regard may have an unfortunate similarity with the false teaching of "name it and claim it" theology. Yes, Jesus encourages us to bring our needs to God (asking him for our daily bread, and presumably the work

21. Villa-Vicencio, *When Prayer Makes News,* 16, 20, 21.

22. Villa-Vicencio, *When Prayer Makes News,* 43, 44.

23. Boesak, "In the Name of Jesus," 39.

24. Shorter, *Prayer in the Religious Traditions,* 24.

25. Tiénou, "Lessons from the Prayer Habits," 270.

which enables us to obtain that bread in an honest, honorable way), but we are not promised that we can get anything we want by simply praying in a certain way. In this regard, we must make a distinction between Christian and non-Christian views of prayer: the Bible does not teach that if we pray in a specific way, we will always get what we ask for. A biblical theology of prayer reveals that God may say "no" to a godly person's request in order to give a different—and superior—good.

For instance, think of Paul's prayer in 2 Cor 12:7–10: Paul fervently desired freedom from the "thorn in the flesh" that was tormenting him. God refused, and Paul learned that in his case, God allowed the "thorn" to remain so that Paul could receive a greater benefit: experiencing God's power being revealed through his weakness. Paul received an answer to his prayer, a clear "no." He also received a greater understanding of God and his ways and a transformed perspective on his own suffering and weaknesses.

Note that Paul needed to be willing to listen for an answer from God. "The success of any conversation calls for a spirit of listening with deep respect to the experience of the other," which in the case of prayer is God himself.[26] It can be easy to fall into the trap of viewing prayer solely as my opportunity to take requests to God, without also realizing God desires me to listen and obey when he speaks. If I fail to listen, I miss an opportunity for prayer to be dialogue.

Of course, communication with God is not only about bringing our requests. Prayer is an opportunity for a large range of things which a person might want to say to God, from confessing sin, to asking for God's justice, to praise, and more. For instance, the prayers of Ghanaian Afua Kuma, an untrained but devout Christian, are full of her own titles for God. She describes Jesus in a variety of ways, including Jesus as the Master of Wisdom, the Fearless one who has pulled the teeth of the viper so that it is powerless, the untiring Porter who carries troubled hearts, and the Chief of Lawyers who brings justice.[27] Her praises honor Jesus for who he is and what he has done, expressing delight in him. Prayer gives us the opportunity to rejoice in our Beloved, just as newlyweds delight in recounting the reasons they love their spouse.

One of the most well-known prayers in the Bible is the Lord's Prayer. Several of the requests in that prayer help us to better understand God's design for prayer. For instance, with regard to the request that God's kingdom

---

26. Magesa, *What Is Not Sacred?*, 114.

27. Kuma, *Jesus of the Deep Forest*, 6, 7, 9, 12.

come on earth, Gomeris highlights, urges a person to "[work] in the present for the coming of the kingdom, in the here and now, and yet [retain] one's hope for the full realization of God's kingdom in the future."[28] We both work, and rely on what God has promised he will do in the future.

Magesa highlights the seemingly mundane nature of some requests in this prayer: "Once again, the Lord's Prayer with its fourfold petition also addresses the same issues of ordinary human needs: food, forgiveness, right thinking, and right living (Matt. 6:9–13; Luke 11:1–4): in a word, *Ubuntu*."[29] *Ubuntu* is an African concept which communicates that "I am, because we are," meaning that an individual's humanity is bound up with the humanity of those around them. We affirm that this truth fits with what Scripture teaches us: Christians do not exist as independent, isolated islands; rather, God views us as different members of the one body of Christ and indeed belong to one another, according to Paul's description of the church (Rom. 12:4–5). Therefore, our prayers should reflect this truth, as we pray not just for our own concerns, but also on behalf of those around us. And as we pray, God mysteriously works through those flawed prayers to transform attitudes, thinking, and actions.

Indeed, prayer helps us transcend our own perspectives and be brought into closer communion with God. But that does not mean that prayer distances us from daily life and the world around us. Rather, prayer can reveal the ties between the heavenly realm and our earthly lives. The Lord's Prayer urges us to take needs that arise in our own lives and our neighbors' lives and place them at God's feet, not to ignore them. Botswanan Musa Dube notes that the Lord's Prayer is not just requests made to God; in praying it, Christians "repeatedly pledge their commitment to and responsibility for the realization of God's will on earth. Thus, it is called the *Lord's* Prayer even though it is women and men who use it, for prayer is an attempt to meet, hear, speak, and work with God."[30]

Therefore, Dube challenges Christians to think about systems that unjustly deprive some of daily food and opportunities for work, as well as economic systems in a time of globalization, which involve crushing debts for many Majority World countries. She argues that as Christians pray for God's will to be done on earth, they are asking God to meet the world's needs. "This, however, does not exempt Christians from responsibility for

28. Domeris, "Jesus, Prayer, and the Kingdom," 115–16.

29. Magesa, *What Is Not Sacred?*, 113.

30. Dube Shomanah, "Praying the Lord's Prayer," 439–50, esp. 439.

these issues. On the contrary, they are to be active participants, who pledge their commitment to the sanctification of God's name through the establishment of God's rule on earth as it is in heaven."[31]

As we pray the Lord's Prayer, if we are willing to listen and reflect, we can hear God replying to us through those same words, telling us what we must do. God is the one who answers prayers, but he may choose to provide the answer through us or another person. John De Gruchy contrasts true piety with false piety, which "reduces Christianity to some private sphere of self-interest, a form of religion without spiritual power or love, an egocentric trip away from social responsibility and discipleship," without a call to obedience and sacrifice.[32] False piety is not what we see in the Lord's Prayer. Gomeris ends his essay with an expanded expression of this prayer:

> In a world where God's name is desecrated, may his name be hallowed. In the midst of political kingdoms at war with each other, may his kingdom come. In societies divided by injustice, class, or race consciousness, where oppression grinds the face of the poor into the dirt, may his will be done. In the midst of a hope for a new tomorrow, may our words and actions anticipate that day as did those of our Lord. In the face of anger and hatred, may we learn to forgive and so be ourselves forgiven.[33]

Gomeris highlights here the distinction between our requests and the broken world in which we currently live, as well as our responsibilities.

What Dube has brought out, and Tiénou affirmed, is that prayer ought to be communal, as we have been reminded by the Lord's Prayer. This prayer—and our own—are not intended to remain individualistic: instead, the Lord's Prayer draws God's people together and teaches us to love those whom we find unlovely, to forgive those who have wronged us even as we seek just ways of living together. We see in the Lord's Prayer that we are called to forgive others, seeking reconciliation with them. God uses prayer to change my heart and spur me to actions that demonstrate love of neighbor; in other words, God can work through my prayer to convict and mobilize me.

Alan Brews urges that "[a]s long as Christians pray 'deliver us from evil,' the evil must be named. To pray 'Thy kingdom come on earth as it is in heaven' is to reject all that contradicts the coming of the kingdom of God. In

---

31. Dube Shomanah, "Praying the Lord's Prayer," 445.

32. De Gruchy, "Prayer, Politics, and False Piety," 103.

33. Domeris, "Jesus, Prayer, and the Kingdom," 124.

South Africa the evil is apartheid."[34] As we pray for God's deliverance, we are responsible to identify and stand against what is evil in the world around us. Further, Dube notes that as we name evil we are also called to repent of our role in perpetuating it. "For Christian communities, nations, institutions and individuals to pray and ask for deliverance from evil in this global age entails repentance accompanied by action, a willingness to hear the Lord's Prayer and to recapture the implications of praying it. To say 'your kingdom come,' to say 'your will be done, on earth as it is in heaven,' is to become responsible partners, guardians of justice, active daughters and sons in the establishment of God's rule in the world."[35] Likewise, a prayer composed for mission work in South Africa prays that Christ

> Will use the Church, his servants:
> We on earth his outstretched hand.
> May his Church in loving service,
> Shown to all whose path is rough,
> Give a clear united witness,
> And proclaim, "Christ is enough!"
> Christ enough to break all barriers;
> Christ enough in peace, in strife;
> Christ enough to build our nation;
> Christ enough for death, for life;
> Christ enough for old and lonely;
> Christ enough for those who fall;
> Christ enough to save the sin-sick;
> Christ enough for one; for all![36]

We see in this prayer communion with God, relying on Christ's sufficiency and presence, and awareness that Christ desires to work through his church. This prayer combines communion, communication, and a commitment to action on the part of the church.

Tiénou notes that in Africa, prayers are appropriate in each and every situation; they are not limited to "religious" contexts but are made before undertaking any action.[37] In Kenya, it is typical for pastors to be invited

---

34. Brews, "When Journalists Do Theology," 74.

35. Dube Shomanah, "Praying the Lord's Prayer," 450.

36. Tutu, *African Prayer Book*, 84.

37. Tiénou, "Lessons from the Prayer Habits," 270.

by their congregants to pray over a newly purchased car or to dedicate a house. There is no situation in which prayer is not viewed as relevant and appropriate. In this regard, the rest of us have much to learn.

Conclusion

What can we conclude about my atheist friend's objections to prayer? He is incorrect that prayer exempts a person from any further action. However, my friend is right that some prayers are answered with a "no." Christians also struggle with God's "no"; yet a key in such times is not to assume that I can or will understand God all the time. While I may not discern the reasons, I am called to trust that he has acted rightly and can bring good out of any evil for his disciples. Tiénou concludes that "Christians everywhere need to keep worship and theology together. If genuine theology is doxology [praise] then a rediscovery of the centrality of prayer is indispensable. This . . . is the major lesson we can learn from prayer" in the African church.[38] Prayer is a precious gift which we ought to treasure.

Yet prayer can get pushed aside as we face responsibilities that can seem more urgent. Reminding ourselves of what prayer is intended to be, and what a gift it is, can help us to value it more highly. At other times, as when my father had cancer, it was a deep need and a feeling of being overwhelmed that can force a person to grow in their prayer life. Arensen admits that he set aside a day for prayer not "because I had well-meaning plans to know God better and improve my spiritual life. I spent that day in prayer out of desperation. God put me in a situation where I could not rely on my own strength or ability, and I needed God."[39] God commands us to seek his face because he knows we need him more than anything else.

Boesak makes his own stance clear: "I believe passionately in prayer. It is an expression of hope and an act of faith. It is to know, not by instinct but through faith, that God is able and willing to respond to the cry of his people. The God and Father of Jesus Christ is the Living One who, in contrast to the false gods of human making, *does* hear, *does* care, *does* act."[40] God works through our prayers in ways we cannot anticipate, bringing transformation to and through the humble person who prays. *Tuvoye*—let us pray!

38. Tiénou, "Lessons from the Prayer Habits," 271.

39. Arensen, *Come Away*, 13.

40. Boesak, "In the Name of Jesus," 9.

Bibliography

Arensen, Shel. *Come Away: How to Have a Personal Prayer Retreat*. Grand Rapids, MI: Kregel, 2003.

Boesak, Allan A. "In the Name of Jesus: A Sermon for 16 June." In *When Prayer Makes News: Churches and Apartheid—A Call to Prayer*, edited by Allan A. Boesak and Charles Villa-Vicencio, 30–40. Philadelphia: Westminster, 1986.

Brews, Alan. "When Journalists Do Theology." In *When Prayer Makes News: Churches and Apartheid—A Call to Prayer*, edited by Allan A. Boesak and Charles Villa-Vicencio, 60–74. Philadelphia: Westminster, 1986.

De Gruchy, John W. "Prayer, Politics, and False Piety." In *When Prayer Makes News: Churches and Apartheid—A Call to Prayer*, edited by Allan A. Boesak and Charles Villa-Vicencio, 97–112. Philadelphia: Westminster, 1986.

Domeris, William R. "Jesus, Prayer, and the Kingdom of God." In *When Prayer Makes News: Churches and Apartheid—A Call to Prayer*, edited by Allan A. Boesak and Charles Villa-Vicencio, 113–24. Philadelphia: Westminster, 1986.

Dube Shomanah, Musa W. "Praying the Lord's Prayer in a Global Economic Era." *The Ecumenical Review* 49 (1997) 439–50.

Kuma, Afua. *Jesus of the Deep Forest: Prayers and Praises of Afua Kuma*. Translated by Fr Jon Kirby. Accra, Ghana: Asempa, 1981.

Magesa, Laurenti. *What Is Not Sacred? African Spirituality*. Nairobi: Acton, 2014.

Mbiti, John S. "*Kwambaza*: An African Prayer for Help." *Dialogue and Alliance* 3 (1989) 14–17.

Peskett, Howard. "Prayer in the Old Testament Outside the Psalms." In *Teach Us to Pray*, edited by D. A. Carson, 19–34. Exeter, UK: Paternoster & Baker, 1990.

Shorter, Aylward. *Prayer in the Religious Traditions of Africa*. New York: Oxford University Press, 1975.

Tiénou, Tite. "Lessons from the Prayer Habits of the Church in Africa." In *Teach Us to Pray: Prayer in the Bible and the World*, edited by D. A. Carson, 268–71. Exeter, UK: Paternoster and Baker, 1990.

Tutu, Desmond. *An African Prayer Book*. New York: Doubleday, 1995.

Villa-Vicencio, Charles. "Introduction." In *When Prayer Makes News: Churches and Apartheid—A Call to Prayer*, edited by Allan A. Boesak and Charles Villa-Vicencio, 15–22. Philadelphia: Westminster, 1986.

———. "Some Refused to Pray: The Moral Impasse of the English-Speaking Churches." In *When Prayer Makes News: Churches and Apartheid—A Call to Prayer*, edited by Allan A. Boesak and Charles Villa-Vicencio, 43–59. Philadelphia: Westminster, 1986.

Conclusion

By JAMES SPENCER, PHD

May I not ask Christian people to begin now to pray for a special outpouring of the Spirit upon every meeting of the conference?
—D. L. MOODY

BEFORE HIS DEATH IN 1899, Dwight Moody issued what would be his last invitation to a conference in Northfield. These conferences, which had quickly outgrown the facilities of the Northfield Seminary for girls, had necessitated the construction of a 2,300-seat auditorium in a town of approximately that size. Commenting on the build, Moody said, "I have always tried to build according to my faith. This time my friends think my faith has carried me away. They do not believe that I shall ever see this building full."[1] Yet, not long after the building was complete, it became apparent that Moody's auditorium was a bit too small with 3,000 people consistently in attendance at the various events held at the site.

Moody's conferences were open to "all of God's people who are interested in the study of his word, in the development of their own Christian lives, in a revival of the spiritual life of the Church, in the conversion of sinners, and in the evangelization of the world."[2] The conferences consisted of preaching, worship, prayer and discernment with the intention of being led by God toward some task, activity, or ministry. Moody believed that when God's people come together to study, worship, pray, and discern, the Holy Spirit will do great things. In his "A Convocation for Prayer," Moody notes his desire to see God's people assemble together "for solemn

---

1. Moody, *Life of Dwight L. Moody*, 373.
2. Moody, *Life of Dwight L. Moody*, 373.

self-consecration, for pleading God's promises, and waiting upon him for a fresh anointment of power from on high."

These conferences were, in many ways, the convergence of Moody's ministry interests insomuch as they brought believers together with the sole intent of hearing from and listening to God. At these conferences, believers were challenged to act on their convictions with regard to evangelism, study, and prayer. Moody desired to see "men and women of average talent" reach the world.

Prayer was central to Moody's understanding of the Christian life and crucial to the accomplishment of the Great Commission. Prayer was not an isolated activity, but intersected with other Christian disciplines such as confession, restitution, Bible study, and adoration. To pray was not to enlist God in one's endeavors, but to open oneself to God's agenda asking him to guide and direct one's paths even if doing so requires the setting aside of one's desires and passions. We must "pray Him to empty us" before "we pray that God would fill us."[3]

We won't become a praying people through a sheer act of will or commitment. As Moody commented to some of those attending his summer conference who wanted to commit to pray for one another daily, "No, don't bind yourselves to do that. Pray for one another, of course, but don't pledge yourselves to do it every day, lest you burden your conscience and make an irksome duty out of what should be a delightful privilege."[4] Prayer is not a chore. It is an acknowledgment that God is really there. He is really active in our lives. He is really sovereign, wise, and benevolent. Prayer is a natural expression that emerges from and contributes to our ever-deepening conviction that God is for us.

If we are to become a people for whom prayer is as essential as breathing, we must not view the discipline of prayer as a habit that we must form. Instead, we must view prayer as a way of life we adopt as we test God's faithfulness (in the Mal 3:10 sense). It is what we do in response to God's active presence among us *and* what we do when we lose sight of that active presence. May we be a people who are constantly aware of God and respond to his ongoing presence among us with the obedience of faith because, as Dwight Moody once said, "In the place God has put us he expects us to shine, to be living witnesses, to be a bright and shining light. While we are here our work is to shine for him."

3. Moody, *Secret Power*, 32.

4. Moody, *Life of Dwight L. Moody*, 367.

Bibliography

Moody, Dwight L. *Secret Power*. Chicago: Revell, 1881.
Moody, William Revell. *The Life of Dwight L. Moody*. Chicago: Revell, 1900.

Printed in the USA
CPSIA information can be obtained
at www.ICGtesting.com
LVHW011508030224
770848LV00003B/61